IF YOU
CLEVER
WHY AREN'T
YOU RICH?

Published by The Big Ideas Library, 2015
Copyright © Jacky Fitt, 2015

First published in Great Britain
First edition 2014

The Big Ideas Library
20 Fountayne Street, York YO31

A CIP catalogue record for this book is available from the British Library.

ISBN 978-0-9929859-0-5

Typeset by Ned Hoste

Printed in by CPI Group (UK)

The Big Ideas Library is the publishing division of The Big Ideas Collective Ltd.

IF YOU'RE SO CLEVER WHY AREN'T YOU RICH?

INTELLECTUAL PROPERTY
10 WAYS
TO TAKE YOUR GENIUS TO THE BANK

ELIZABETH WARD

big ideas library®

This book is dedicated to my mum – a midwife who brought the breath of life to many and was a breath of fresh air to everyone who knew her.
Marion Elizabeth Ward
24 September 1922 -17 May 2011

It is also dedicated to my wonderful friends who have supported me in writing this book.
You know who you are!
Thank you.

Contents

Introduction

I'm indebted to a very dear friend for the title of this book. The phrase "If you're so clever why aren't you rich" was, in fact, a family jibe used by my friend on his two sisters, both of whom were academically, if not financially, very successful in their careers. But in this case the title could well be used by any number of businesses who have great ideas but struggle to make money from them. This book is unashamedly focused on those who **do** want to make a fortune from their ideas but don't know where to start.

Containing lots of practical information about Intellectual Property (IP) and its application in business, this book is for start-ups, small to medium enterprises (SMEs) and those businesses who are looking to dig deep into new territories to future proof their businesses. It is for those ambitious business owners, directors and entrepreneurs who want to benefit from their IP right from the get-go and/or strengthen their business before an initial public offering (IPO) or trade sale within the next five years.

This book is NOT is a substitute for taking expert legal advice. It's a guide; it will help you ask the right questions and point you in the right direction. It will add value to your business and increase your knowledge bank. "The man who uses himself as a lawyer has a fool for a client." In an increasingly complicated and litigious world, this saying has never been more apt.

The Business of Brand

Ever wondered what would happen if *Nike®* or *Adidas®* took their names and logos off trainers? Would you be left with just another pair of trainers? Would you recognise the build quality or styling of the trainer in the absence of the name? I know that I'd struggle with that conundrum.

> *"Within every brand is a product, but not every product is a brand."* David Ogilvy

Do you ever give any thought to food packaging? The style of the packaging, its name and position on the supermarket shelf? Do you wonder why food manufacturers give such thought to colour, name, and styling of what they sell? One style is used to sell a "value" product and another to sell an upmarket version of the same with usually similar contents. The same also applies to drinks manufacturers who make sure that bottles, labels and brand names have a particular "look" that entices their customers to buy them.

The "look" of such goods is carefully researched – and a different "look" will attract different buyers according to label design, brand name, type face and message to the consumer. Clever marketers can carefully construct the look of a product to attract a certain age group or a particular audience.

Did you know that pharmaceutical companies patent not only the drug, but also the way the drug is made? They also patent incremental improvements in the drug, such as an improvement in the way the drug is delivered to the human body or the way it is manufactured. Clever technologists will "landscape" the patents already filed, months **before** they undertake any research and development (R&D). After all, where is the sense in researching technology that is already ring fenced by a third party? Yet many businesses do just that!

The packaging industry and some toy manufacturers review their designs and register the "look" of a concept where they think a product will become a best seller. Indeed, the *Tetrapak* carton style of packaging, which revolutionised the packaging industry for liquids, was originally patented. Those patents expired years ago and are now long gone; however, Tetrapak is still a successful packaging company. Do you ever wonder what made it a longer term success?

Digital and Data

The words, layout, metadata and links of a website, as well as its domain name can greatly contribute to how easily a website is found on Google and therefore the traffic and volume of business it conducts. If someone slavishly copies the copyright of the website, including headings, metadata and format then the website owner **can and will** lose lines of inquiry and profit overnight.

Some businesses make a business out of creating super databases. Take the British Horse Racing Board (BHB) and the quantity and quality of data it produces on horses, riders, trainers and owners. The data it creates is of huge use to the gambling industry. Even modest businesses can have very valuable databases.

These databases are of particular interest to some buyers, even though the buyer may not be at all interested in the core business. Some of my biggest and fastest growing clients have made significant money using computerised databases that extract key information, which can provide amazing accuracy and detail in respect of consumer trends or data for Government statistics. You see a database isn't just a customer list or random information – it is a map, a landscape that when interpreted correctly forms vital data for many businesses. How do you navigate the waters of your industry? Do you use the shore as a reference point, the stars or a GPS? You see winning the business race isn't about sailing the boat faster; it is about sailing the boat as safely and as quickly as you can in the right direction. Information can be used as a powerful directional tool.

Hiding in plain sight

What the BHB and other businesses are doing (sometimes without understanding it) is acknowledging the intellectual property in their businesses and making sure their investment is both protected and commercialised, thereby creating, not only a revenue stream, but also a strategic tool for growth. Sadly, however, quite a number of businesses simply don't recognise or see the value of mapping and documenting data to differentiate themselves from their competitors and miss out on creating a unique competitive edge.

It's high time we all got IP savvy, but why is it taking us so long to work out how to invest and exploit our wealth by creating intangible assets?

Why is the UK so poor at understanding and making use of its IP?

Why are our banks and senior people in industry and Government so ignorant of the value and importance of industrial IP? The answer is fairly straight forward – many people just don't recognise, let alone identify or value the IP in their businesses. Company executives may acknowledge the research and development departments, or marketing and creative departments in their organisations; however, most CEO's want to move straight to selling products and services to generate an income stream. They fail to recognise the importance of getting their IP in good, systematic or 'apple pie' order so that, not only can they protect the business from piracy and general copying, but also that they can generate long term future income streams from licensing and other forms of commercialisation, such as distribution agreements, licensing, agency or franchising. Many R&D departments don't capture the innovation they create, nor do they have systems in place to capture and review creation and that's where they're losing out. **The four key IP mantras for modern businesses must be:**

1. Identify

2. Protect

3. Commercialise

4. Defend

Historically, businesses have actually failed in many respects to give IP any thought what so ever. Finance directors and banks have always been quick off the mark to recognise the value and invest heavily in bricks and mortar. This relies too much on old market values that no longer exist. Sadly, investment in the IP of a company has often been seen as a "drain" on company resources - a negative on the balance sheet and not the foundation of the company's future. Simply put, IP is not treated as an asset or an investment – just an expense. Even, during times of recession which has seen the wholesale collapse and devaluing of many bricks and mortar based property portfolios there is still a fundamental lack of commitment in UK businesses to acknowledge and sell its biggest asset – its IP. Meanwhile overseas, they've been quick to catch on.

The Second Industrial Revolution

In 1963 UK Prime Minister Harold Wilson coined the phrase, "white heat of the technological revolution." In fact, what he was talking about at the time were the huge post war advances in manufacturing techniques in the UK. Wilson knew that the UK had to face an ever changing future and that if it did not keep up then it would simply die. What he actually said was:

"The Britain which is going to be forged in the white heat of the revolution will be no place for restrictive practices or for outdated methods on either side of industry."

His mission was in fact to get the UK's industry leaders and workforce to accept new ways of doing things; to adapt to, what is in, truth, the new or second industrial revolution and it's happening right now. **Why Now?**

So why, in the first half of the new Millennium, are we experiencing the second Industrial Revolution? First of all you have to look at the first Industrial Revolution of the 18th and 19th century and its impact. The first Industrial Revolution started in the UK and then spread worldwide. It affected every aspect of life; it was a major change in society at every level and it heralded unprecedented growth and prosperity.

The prime movers of change were the introduction of power to industrial processes (steam engines, water power and the combustion engine) and mechanisation of equipment (cotton spinning, the printing press and making iron). Today's revolution is largely silent by comparison. Technological leaps in IT, computing, microprocessors and infrastructure changes have propelled the workplace into something that would not have been recognised even 50 years ago. In the UK, our telecoms, aviation, broadcast, pharmaceutical, music, engineering and transport industries to name but a few are world beating. It staggers me that we are so quiet about our talents. What is also a crying shame is that so few businesses recognise the value in what they do, especially on the world stage.

In this book I intend to demonstrate to you the real return on investment in IP in the UK; why it should be placed at the heart of our economy and practice, and why it is the future of our economic growth.

Stand by to be amazed by what I can demonstrate to you and how you can benefit financially. If you are not as passionate as I am about releasing your business IP potential by the end of this book, then I've failed!

Step 1
Intellectual Property:
What It Is and What It's Worth in UK Plc

First of all let's look at the more obvious areas in which UK Plc excels itself for its "Intellectual Property" (IP). A leading player for many years in automotive technological innovation, the UK car industry is a good place to begin. It is still the home of Formula One racing and all the research that goes into making cars faster, safer, greener and leaner. Much of what the industry creates, it effectively syndicates or licenses out. So, although one company may make a better air bag, that technology is shared. Thereby generating an income for the original company who invested in the R&D to create it. Provided the technology is genuinely shared, and the monopoly created by the IP is used to everyone's benefit, then it is usually a win-win situation.

It isn't just car manufacturers who are at the cutting edge of research in the UK. Companies such as ACAL Energy, based on the Wirral in the North West, are leading the way in fuel cell technology to help power tomorrow's world. I'd always mistakenly believed that fuel cells were huge batteries which stored energy. In fact they are their own little combustion engines, generating power from hydrogen and oxygen to create an electrical current, which can indeed be stored like a battery and used to power things. The waste product from this process is water.

The Japanese have always appeared to lead research into fuel cells and many believe they are world beaters in this arena. What ACAL Energy have done, however, is move into PEM or proton exchange membrane technology. In simple terms the ACAL team took know-how from the Wirral based soap industry and used soap oxidising agents to deliver more power (oxygen) to the fuel cells they were developing. Simple but clever applications of two already known technologies creating a new one - genius.

In a way this is often what inventors do. Look at Mr Dyson and some of his brilliant remodelling of existing technology to make it better. Thanks to Dyson, the UK plc has created new hand held vacuums, hand driers, heating and cooling fans. For more about this kind of IP see Step 2 and read Professor Geoff Tucker's comments on recognising what is new in a business. But, before we leave the subject of power generation, it is worth mentioning that UK technology and scientists have made significant contributions to the technology, safety and efficacy of fracking for shale gas. The UK oil industry has also made significant technological advances over the years – even though on a world stage, we're a "bit player" in terms of production.

On a more consumer minded level, the UK is known worldwide for its music and creative industry. Look at the graphics and software we produce for web pages, our computer games industry, our TV dramas, and add up what they mean to the UK economy. This "scepter'd isle" as Shakespeare (another great UK export) put it, is rich with genius and talent. Historically, we've always been a nation of creators and inventors. James Hargreaves's Spinning Jenny and Richard Arkwright's water powered mills changed the face of the cotton industry. From their genius inventions dozens of others followed, including James Watt's steam driven water pumps that were soon adapted to power other machines and mechanise production.

Bringing us more up to date, we have the likes of Sir Tim Berners-

Lee, the British Physicist credited with creating the worldwide web. The first superfast Maglev (magnetic levitation) train was in fact built and run in Birmingham; however, it seems it has taken the Germans and the Chinese to improve the technology to make it a commercial reality. Sadly, this appears to be often the case. Take for example the microwave oven. The original work on microwaves was done by scientists working on magnetrons in Britain's UK radar system. Those working on these machines both in the UK and later in the USA "cooked" or rather blew up food in front of the beam! Potatoes, eggs and popcorn were sacrificed NOT in the name of science but because blowing things up in front of your colleagues is vastly amusing, if rather messy. Guess what? The people who made the first microwave ovens were not British. Yet again the commercialisation of technology was seized by other countries such as the USA and Japan. Whilst we may be wonderful designers, inventors and creators of technology, time after time in the last 50 years we've been appallingly bad at taking the next step and actually making money out of our original ideas. Let's hope that from now on we can educate people at every level to support our creatives so that the wealth and business opportunities benefit the UK.

The Clicks Not Bricks Workplace

Now, let's look at where we are today – where are the companies that have real IP value? Some of these companies work in what I call "bricks" or traditional areas such as mining, building and infrastructure. However, many I term as "clicks companies". By way of example, these would include IBM, Microsoft, Nokia, Apple and Google. Other industries would include the healthcare industries such as GSK and Pfizer. These companies have <u>huge</u> portfolios of intellectual property

– indeed IP assets are what they are built on. Even less obvious is the huge value that IP has delivered to industries such as banking, insurance and the oil industry. Our financial service industries have made vast improvements in the delivery of products and value to shareholders by investing in IT infrastructures, encryption, software platforms for trade and bespoke software solutions.

The petrochemical industry is much more profitable because it has researched into improved fuel additives and improved production techniques. By the way – a lot of the R&D done in those industries is done over here in the UK, either in specialised technology centres or in universities and their associated institutes. What ALL of these successful companies have done is embrace the value of their IP. A number of them continually overhaul their IP strategies and direction and they do that for a reason – IT ADDS VALUE TO THEIR COMPANY. IP rights, if properly managed, incentivise the creators of such rights and CREATE WEALTH.

Even though it is glaringly obvious to me that UK companies need an IP strategy, and many of them have spent millions on their IP, we still have vast numbers of people in the UK who just can't see that value. I'm regularly told by business owners that their accountant has told them that their IP can't be valued, or put on the balance sheet and that investing in a patent portfolio is no more than a drain on resources, rather than an investment in the future of the company. This view is simply WRONG! To help explain my point of view, take, for example, a number of little known facts:

Little Known Facts about IP

1. **Your IP can be valued and put on the balance sheet.** The calculations are often difficult and are sometimes undertaken by specialist accountants, but the important fact to take away is that IP can be valued. Putting it on the balance sheet requires further advice – but <u>is</u> possible. If you want to look at this in a simple way, think about taking away your main company or trading name and then look at who (if anyone) would recognise your business; or more importantly, walk through the door and buy from you. In the same way, if your main technology wasn't protected by a patent or similar know-how, then how unique would you be? If you didn't protect your database what would stop your competitors from marching in and stealing your customer base? Not protecting your IP is akin to leaving the Crown Jewels on the pavement outside the Tower of London- how long do you think they would remain there untouched?

2. **Your IP can be mortgaged or "charged" in the same way that bricks and mortar property can have a charge attached to it.** The mortgage charge can be registered at Companies House and in some circumstances the Intellectual Property office just as a mortgage on your property would be recorded at the Land Registry or Companies House. However, you can't mortgage it and raise funds against it without it having some form of value. Alternatively, what would your bricks and mortar property be worth if it had a load of squatters in it who didn't pay any rent and weren't making any contribution to the upkeep of the property? The same is true of copied IP assets – they're devalued.

3. **Licenses of your trade marks, patents and registered design rights can and should be registered** at the various intellectual property offices round the world in order to formally record the interest of the rights owner (the licensor) and the user of the rights (the licensee). Those licensees should generate value to the licensor by way of income streams from royalties. If the IP is being used without permission then you need to ask why this is occurring and what you can do to stop money from seeping away from your business. The license revenue can be valued and these types of contracts will add massively to your bottom line and the value of your business. A good licensing portfolio can also be used by some banks for lending purposes. Good contracts will greatly increase the value of your company, and are vital if you are seeking to sell the company or obtain investment. Who is interested in buying a company, where its main sources of licensing revenue is drafted on a cigarette packet? Or where the contracts are drafted by an amateur?

4. **The amount you spend on registration of your rights is probably just the start of any valuation process.** The value increases depending on a number of complex factors. Such as how many licensees you have, how competitive the market is and how long your registered rights have to run. The value of your IP rights can vary from year to year and you need a constant review process. If you own property, the rental income on your portfolio can and will change. It is the same with your IP.

5. **The deliberate undermining of IP, either through counterfeit products, or look-alike products is a serious issue.** IP rights must be properly defended and licenses fully audited to make

sure that their value isn't dissipated. In an economic downturn copying always increases – what are you doing about such criminal activity? It isn't just your short term profit you will lose, it is customers and therefore £££, who won't come back when they see your designer items being touted on the streets.

6. **The banks and other institutions are only just learning how to securitize IP assets**, - convert IP into a marketable asset to raise cash or attract investment. Whilst many understand how the process works for registered IP rights such as patents or trade marks, few have got their heads round unregistered rights such as software. In times of austerity when banks are tying themselves in knots making lending as difficult as possible, my personal view is that Government and industry champions need to lead a change in attitude. The banks need more real business people on their boards and, dare I say it, a lot more women! They need to relax some of their more silly lending criteria and embrace and understand IP as an asset base.

The point is that ALL IP has a value! Ignore it at your peril.

Big businesses such as Shell, BP and GSK, to name but a few, all have an IP strategy and with good reason. They spend millions of pounds making sure they're at the cutting edge of business and, as such, need to protect their position. for very good financial reasons.

IP, Tax, Investment and the Role of Government

It isn't just me who bangs the drum for IP in the UK. The Confederation of British Industry (CBI) - to name but one organisation - is lobbying hard for the UK to be the destination of choice for IP creation and development. Unlike the first Industrial Revolution, we now have several rivals including Germany, France and Canada who have strong research bases and are encouraging IP creation through financial incentives and support from government. The UK Government has already made changes to encourage businesses to invest in their IP. My view is that they haven't done enough.

By way of example, tax relief is available for R&D. The rules of such schemes are not always that straight forward and it is always worthwhile taking expert advice. In brief, however, R&D tax credits are available to any company that pays corporation tax. They fall into two main schemes. One scheme is for SMEs and one is for larger companies. The two important criteria are that any R&D must be linked to the existing business or one that the business is diversifying into, and that the business must own the IP. BUT what many companies don't know is how broad these tax reliefs are. R&D tax credits can be claimed on everything from staff costs, to the creation of computer software and even subcontracted out R&D! (Ownership is covered in more detail later in this book, as it is a key part of the IP process and strategy to ascertain ownership.) Claiming your tax credits can add straight to your bottom line – so why is it THE most under claimed tax relief in the UK?

The UK Government has also set up a so called "Patent Box" tax relief scheme whereby businesses that make profits from patents (and **not** other types of IP) will benefit from paying only 10% corporation tax. This has the potential to bring some overseas R&D company investment to the UK. The Patent Box is seen by many as central to the future wealth and attractiveness of their businesses on the world stage.

In addition to these measures I'd like to see low rates of corporation tax to ALL IP rich businesses. In this way we'd encourage investment from overseas into the UK by way of big brand owners setting up over here and by providing benefits to our software, media and associated industries. The message is clear to government – if you are serious about creating greater wealth from IP then create a "Royalty Box" regime whereby all IP rich businesses can benefit. After all, business these days is global and operates from any number of locations. The UK must encourage businesses and individuals to feel we have a stable and favourable tax regime for them to step into.

One of the other key roles of Government is to create and encourage excellent infrastructure. There is a pressing need for the UK to be enabled at every level to use first rate IT systems. This means ensuring that every member of the public has access to high speed networks and IT systems that work. Many of the UK Government's own systems are way behind where they should be and that in itself makes them inefficient and slow. Indeed, some of the worst examples of IT procurement were Government projects and millions of pounds of tax payers' money has been wasted on projects which were badly managed, failed to deliver the specification and functionality required by the end users or more worryingly, simply never saw the light of day. If you weren't already convinced by the true value of IP to UK businesses, then consider these economic facts taken from a November 2009 CBI report:

Pharmaceuticals

1. The UK's pharmaceutical or "pharma" industry contributes £9 billion to the UK economy but, more importantly, it creates £12 billion in exports, employs 70,000 in the UK with a further 250,000 in related industries.

Chemicals

2. The UK chemicals sector turns over £50 billion and directly employs 214,000.

Software

3. The UK's creative industries account for 8.2% of the UK's GDP – over £100 billion a year and expect to grow at 4% pa until 2013.

Games

4. The UK's computer games industry generates £2 billion of sales annually and employs 21,000.

Print

5. The UK's magazine and journal industry contributes £5.7 billion to the UK economy.

Aerospace

6. The UK aerospace industry turned over £20 billion in 2007, employed 120,000 and spent £2.74 billion on R&D.

Brands

7. The UK has around 1 million people directly employed in the creation and management of brands and makes an estimated contribution of £18.6 billion to the economy.

People - the Heart of any Business

Finally, a word on people and the IP business. This point is covered in much more detail later on in the book; however, it is worth saying first and foremost that the creation of IP needs good creative people. Again the UK is rich with talent. The research undertaken in our universities often proves world beating and the UK is well known for its engineers, chemists, designers and software developers. Many of the UK's universities now have "cluster" type business parks around them. The fact of the matter is that many people from all over the world like living in the UK and those involved in the creation of IP need to be nurtured in a supportive and creative environment.

The business park clusters create such an environment, and employees are happy to stay near to centres of research and connections. A stable political environment, good state schooling, healthcare and welfare systems all directly contribute to encouraging overseas researchers and investors to come to the UK. If investors like the UK as a country and it offers a relatively low personal and corporate tax regime, then they will stay and contribute to the economy.

If you want to see how to reverse this, – then look at what happened in France throughout 2012/13. The French Government introduced a tax level of 75% for the so called "super-rich". Hmmm, let me see – the super rich. They're the ones that you want to STAY in the country aren't they? Not jet set off to another country because of punitive taxes. When they stay put they build businesses, invest and spend their money IN the country they live in.

My view is that such individuals need rewarding in the same way that entrepreneurs need rewarding for investing their money into IP rich businesses. I would therefore like to see tax breaks and incentives for anyone who wants to live in the UK and create IP either directly through research or investment in IP businesses. If we don't do that we face the loss of good researchers and investors to other countries and therefore suffer a net loss to the UK. My observation of many researchers who weren't born in the UK is that they are often much more business savvy than their UK equivalents. Losing key people in any organisation can cause a direct hit to the bottom line. Equally, staff who can't react to change or collaboratively work can mean whole organisations stagnate and subsequently implode.

Step 2
Mining, Extracting and Processing IP

One of the key problems in many businesses is identifying the IP and then sorting the useful and valuable from the expendable and deciding how to manage both types of assets – always within a budget. So let's start with a few key guidelines:

1. Brands

In any organisation the first thing people think of is the name of that organisation and the association that name or brand has to the consumer. Some brands deliver some obvious messages. British Airways® has always been seen as a premier airline. Ryanair®, however, deliver a "value brand" message in the same way that Aldi® does. Brands are the core of any business and the goodwill associated with them is the essence of what is "bought" by the consumers. To quote an IP lawyers' often used phrase, the goodwill of a brand is "the attractive force that brings in custom." Brands make a business "sticky" – i.e. if consumers like the brand then customers come back again and again. Of course the brand has to deliver on whatever promise it is associated with. Most businesses also have brands associated with particular goods and services that they deliver. So, for example, Microsoft® has a program called PowerPoint® and Marks and Spencer's® have their Autograph® range of women's clothing. These names identify and differentiate the goods and services provided by the main name. Also, brands aren't just written words or logos, for example the jingle associated with an advertising campaign could also be a brand, as can and is most packaging. So the obvious start point in any evaluation of IP is the business' brands.

2. Technology

Although you may be forgiven for thinking that the technology in a business is obvious, sadly it is not always the case. A key product or process may be patented. Alternatively the technology could be kept as a trade secret or could simply be the know-how in doing something. Many UK businesses don't use the patenting route to protect their technology. In fact, what they often do is use a combination of know-how and secrecy to stop their competitors from finding out just what it is they are doing that is so unique. This is certainly used in highly competitive sectors such as Formula 1 racing, as the different teams work hard to keep certain technology secret and away from their competitors. This works well until the technology enters the public domain. Specialist know-how also often leaves with key members of staff, sometimes with disastrous consequences.

The early Venetian glass makers had an interesting attitude to employees who knew about their very lucrative and unique glassmaking techniques. Once you were an apprenticed glass maker in Renaissance Venice you weren't allowed to leave the province. In fact, if you did, the Doges sent out a team of men to hunt you down and kill you. An interesting and effective way of keeping a trade secret... Clearly this wouldn't work today, even though many of my more frustrated clients wish it would!

3. Designs

For functional designs, such as the creation of a new pair of sunglasses or piece of furniture, in general the period of legal protection is short lived and minimal. It is possible to use the Registered Design route for designs that have so called "eye appeal". If you invent a better looking consumer item, then registration is a route you SHOULD consider. Continual improvement in product design is often central to making things work better, cleaner, faster, more attractively or whatever. It is quite possible to set out an audit trail to improve the uniqueness and commercial advantage of designs in business. Design rights tend to be the Cinderella subject for business as they're usually overlooked and often ignored from a valuation perspective. The really savvy business owner can, however, use them in combination with patent rights to make the business better protected and a product much more attractive.

4. Copyrights

For many consulting businesses the biggest asset they have is in the material they produce by way of manuals, guides, precedents and increasingly things such as websites, videos and DVD materials. What is often overlooked in many businesses, however, is the value of the software, databases, CAD designs and similar copyright material. Increasingly, high tech businesses rely on things such as data modelling or sophisticated software reporting systems. For example data modelling can reduce traffic jams and deliver personalised medication; it can also deliver customers to buyers in the blink of an eye! Such systems often go unrecognised in terms of their contribution to the business as an asset. Businesses often miss out on reclaiming tax by way of R&D tax credits on these software systems too. Imagine, if you can, the bottom line value that internet banking has added to the profits of the High Street banks, or the trading floor of the stock markets. A good way of truly adding value to many businesses is to use software systems which improve the efficiency of processes and, for example, keep customer or supplier records up to date and accurate. Think of the way Amazon and similar businesses have delivered easy to use applications that simply add more opportunities to sell more products!

Copyrights are also of huge value in the software and web based businesses, where graphics and clever functionality make products unique and highly sought after. A good example of this is smart phone applications or 'apps'. Hail a cab in London and pay for it on your phone. How smart is that? The same is true of good designs in the clothing, footwear and consumer goods. Even the copyright in packaging makes products more desirable and hence increases their value for the business. There is always something very special about unwrapping a Chanel fragrance from its iconic black and white signature packaging, or jewellery from Tiffany in its easily identifiable pale blue box.

Incentivising Staff to Help

Whilst most staff are only too willing to help with an IP review that will help the company, it is always worthwhile thinking about letting them know what is in it for them. I'm indebted to Dinesh Jotwani for his experiences whilst working at Symantec in India. Symantec found it difficult to motivate staff to disclose their research work as part of the mining of IP process. It wasn't that they didn't care, it was just that they were researchers, and there seemed little point in disclosure, as it didn't really impact their daily lives.

In-house lawyer Dinesh devised a clever scheme whereby staff were not only financially rewarded for disclosures but where their inventions were also publicly recognised and publicly rewarded. Dinesh devised awards ceremonies for the staff and the company. In fact what gave the staff the greatest morale boost was knowing that their work was appreciated and of value. In this way identifying what IP had been created became a cornerstone of their business. A simple idea but how often do we ever think about the process and officially thank our staff for their R&D work at every level?

You may also like to bear in mind that some staff just don't like change and will resist an IP review for that reason alone. Also remember that outside advisors may not be objective - especially if they believe their income will drop as a result of a review. Objective advice may cost more, but it may also pay dividends in the longer term.

Improving What's Already There

There are lots of ways of looking at improving the IP in your business to make it more successful and attractive to customers. Improvement doesn't have to be earth shattering for it to count. One of the things that used to really grate with me when I worked in big law firms doing due diligence on companies ready for investment, was how they had overlooked their IP altogether. So often they had lost vital opportunities. For example, it was common to see businesses that had raced on to commercialise a product without investigating whether or not it could or should be patented. Alternatively, they'd had bad advice and been told patenting wasn't possible for their product or was too expensive or was in some way not appropriate.

Misinformation and poor advice abound — why people listen to those who have NO expertise or real background as a practitioner is beyond me. If you were really ill you'd want to see a specialist — not just your GP! By the time the investment community/banks/investors were crawling over the proposition, the opportunity to file and gain a strategic position and monopoly on the IP technology had passed. Understandably, investors would see this as short sighted, devalue the company and reduce their investment or not progress it further. The same applies at a trade sale.

Why buy a company that has been so badly run that it has neglected its IP?

First Of All File Your Patent

Even if products are already patented or filing is applied for, then it may be worthwhile to look at creating a patent "thicket" around the product and the process, thereby deterring competitors and obtaining an advantage on incremental improvements in technology. Companies such as Apple, Shell, Dyson and Siemens routinely file even the most modest improvements and "add on" applications to ensure they stay ahead of the game. This strategy is common in Japan, Germany, Korea and elsewhere but is often dismissed out of hand by UK companies.

It's important to note that the window of opportunity to file is narrow. You can always discontinue filing a patent but what you can't do is regain the novelty aspect of it and then retrospectively file when you think it may be commercial.

The only country which allows patenting of products after they've been commercialised is the USA and even then there are strict limits to the timescales and opportunities. I've nagged many a start-up company or SME to get their core technology filed as a patent as soon as possible. One such company I acted for had some key mobile telephony applications, which I knew could and should be patented. Their well qualified business advisor had told them it wasn't possible but that was incorrect advice. After some persuasion on my part they sought advice from a patent attorney I'd suggested and they filed their first application. Some six months later their main investor revealed that one of the key reasons why he had invested was because of the strength of having a patent in that area of technology. The simple point is that a patent makes that 'space' yours and yours alone. Unless your competition can invent around it, then you can keep them away. A 'thicket' of patents works even better.

Another company, which initially failed to spot the unique value in what it was doing, was a University of Sheffield spin out company called Simcyp Limited – now part of Certara. The academics at Sheffield were doing some amazing in vitro drug modelling. Their idea took existing population databases and, using some clever algorithms, created software that modelled the effects of drugs on different humans and human populations, without the need for live testing on people. The underlying premise was that if you could test an aircraft wing using simulation software, then with the right data you could use the same type of modelling concepts for drug testing. Hence Simcyp was born.

Simcyp's Professor Geoff Tucker later admitted, "We didn't see what was new in what we created. We didn't recognise that we had created valuable IP. It is laughable now but at the time we just thought we had taken two existing bits of technology and merged them and there was nothing new about it. When Liz said we had made ground breaking new technology and explained it we finally got the message. However, sadly, that was after we'd had an issue over ownership of the software. Luckily after an expensive court battle back in 2003 we eventually resolved that problem in our favour."

Trading on Trade Marks

Whilst there is not anything like the same time pressure on registering trade marks as there is for filing patents, this too is often overlooked. Frequently portfolios of trade marks aren't managed properly meaning cover is not obtained in key countries or in the right classes. Whilst working on one transaction years ago, I cross referenced all the trade marks in one organisation only to find that many of their leading brands had no protection at all internationally. We also found out that what had been registered was registered in the wrong company name. I had only been instructed when the deal to sell the company was concluding. Sadly my exercise for the seller was too little too late – the company already had a buyer. A brief review exercise by the purchaser revealed that the costs of rectification of this muddle would be around £50,000. With 12 hours to go before signing off on the deal, the sellers had to decrease the value of the business by £50,000. In fact the figures were not at all accurate but with such little time left I had little opportunity to improve the situation for the seller. **They took a major and entirely avoidable hit on the disposal price.**

Reviewing your trade mark portfolio for cover well before a sale is, however, only part of the story. Trade marks can be logos, jingles, colours and even smells! A review of a company's key brands often flushes out several opportunities to broaden the cover, review or sell old brands or even discontinue the renewals on brands no longer required. Such an audit can often reveal the opportunity to strengthen a brand by adding products for sale under that brand – a process known as **brand extension.** A well known example of this would be Virgin®. We now have Virgin Trains, Virgin Airways, Virgin Money and so on. A brand review can also be an opportune moment to seek strategic help from other brands to offer a combination of brand promises by teaming with other brand owners and offering something unique to the consumer. Finally, packaging plays a key role in the attractiveness of goods these days. What does your packaging say about your brand? Are you positioned as Tesco's Luxury or Value brand?

Due Diligence on Design

Designs briefly fall into two broad categories. Unregistered and Registered Designs (RDs). Unregistered designs is an area of IP that is poorly understood. The "design" of something could be the product in whole or in part. So, for example, a fancy shaped light bulb would have a design in the entire product, or in just parts of it – say the filament or the shape of the bulb. Components of design which have to "fit" together, such as the bayonet fitting are excluded from design right. This is called the "must fit, must match" exception.

Businesses involved in manufacturing products constantly review their design processes to improve functionality; however, real strides are often made when companies get to grips with the "look" aspect of a product. The new styled *Mini*® is a great example. Launched in 1959, the original design created by Sir Alexander Issigonis became an iconic design. BMW® recreated the look and feel of the original Mini and created a new improved version, which has proved a best seller. Ironically, Issigonis felt that other designs of cars such as the Morris Minor were better cars as, at the time, the Mini was manufactured on such a low budget. Indeed the Mini was truly a budget car! He also famously failed his maths exams three times calling pure mathematics "the enemy of creative genius."

A more up to date example is the Apple *iPod*® There were other MP3 players on the market well before the iPod; however, Apple's genius for design and ease of use created a whole new demand for this type of technology and accelerated their desirability.

Protecting the Look of a Product.

Registered Designs protect the "look and feel" of a product. Provided the design is new it is possible to register the design and protect it for up to 25 years. Some toy manufacturers routinely file applications for toys they feel are likely best sellers. This works by keeping the competition away from their toys "look".

The same also applies to say car accessories, sunglasses and garden furniture. Few smaller companies use the Registered Design process, which is a shame as it provides useful protection for products, especially in the early years when successful products hit the market and get copied. One of my clients - Off the Wall Limited of Bradford - have very successfully used the Registered Design route to protect their innovative TV stands. The directors who run Off the Wall knew when they set up that whilst there were plenty of TV stands around, none of the existing ones were particularly eye catching. As a result they set about creating new and attractive TV stands which proved immediately popular. Now they're exporting them!

The healthcare industry is also a good example of a sector that often uses designs on new aids for the disabled and so on. Again, registration gives vital protection and adds value to their product lines. Another client of ours, Daily Care, has used design right protection to protect a unique range of wheel chairs and beds with useful and attractive design features.

Some businesses also use their copyright material in the form of literature, film and music to generate income. An obvious example of this would be the music or broadcast industry. Programme makers routinely make programmes for say the BBC, but then syndicate or licence the programmes and indeed the programme formats to other broadcasters. Writers too will commonly author a book and then adapt the book for theatre performances and so on. Each time a new format is created, then so is a new copyright. So for example the Harry Potter novels have created new copyrights in the film versions, costumes and character merchandise and whatever else may flow from the original books. **The real long term value, as Disney will tell you, is in the value of merchandising or licensing the rights from books and movies.**

A great example of combining copyrights and licensing rights is to build incremental incomes based on multiple copyrights. Take the well known chef Jamie Oliver. Clearly, his empire includes restaurants and charitable work, but it also includes the production of books, cookware and TV programmes. It is even possible to get the Jamie Oliver app for your Apple *iPhone*® with recipes on. I know. I have it on mine…

Individuals such as Jamie Oliver and David Beckham can also make substantial amounts of money with product endorsements and licensing deals, not only for products with their names on, but also for the endorsement of advertising campaigns. Leveraging contracts for TV and sports personalities through image rights is BIG Business, and it is now possible for them to register their image rights using legislation in Guernsey. They then use that protection in the UK. The big brand owners are quick to catch on to who is in the public eye and who will provide the same brand values as they do. Think Gary Lineker and *Walker's Crisps*®. This can of course have disastrous consequences if the person giving the endorsement falls away from the brand values, as top golfer, USA's Tiger Woods will testify after his unfortunate and all too public fall from grace.

Reviewing the Assets

Having an IP portfolio is a bit like having a wardrobe. You have to move on/recycle or dispose of the clothes you don't need. Concentrate on what will never fit you again, is out of style or was never your best outfit and decide what to do with it! Just because you can't find a use for it doesn't mean it has no value, and might find a nice new home with owners that care about it and want it. Seriously though, you'd be surprised at the number of businesses that simply labour on with old software that is no longer delivering what it should, or big businesses who simply pay renewal fees on their IP assets without assessing either the way forward or deciding that it isn't viable any longer to continue the process.

There are opportunities to sell IP either at auction (these types of auctions are rare but do exist) or to try and find a broker who can make a match between buyer and seller. By way of example, it may be that the domain names you bought and the patents you filed are no longer where your business is heading. Alternatively, a review of your patent strategy may show that your key markets weren't where you thought they were and there is little point in continuing to prosecute them, pay translation costs and renewal fees.

Whilst this type of housekeeping is relatively simple, few businesses strategically review their portfolio in this way.

It could also be that your technology now has new opportunities in different fields of use. How about technology that measures fluid flows in pipes. This technology could have a medical application for measuring blood flow in blood vessels. A new combined application IS often new IP!

The key point I'm making is that a strategic review can achieve three important objectives:

1. It can save you filing fees and help you focus.

2. It can generate an income through the licensing/disposal routes.

3. It strengthens what you're already doing and gives you direction.

These lessons are lost in many businesses until, of course, they hit the pain point and want to sell the business or keep the competition out and maintain shareholder value.

Ownership

One of the biggest problems I see with IP in businesses boils down to ownership. In my mind it is simple. A ship only has one captain. What they say goes. It is the same with IP. You can only have one owner – and not several. Joint ownership usually spells disaster for a variety of reasons. I get cross when people suggest joint ownership. It is far better to have one person have legal title with other interested parties having fully formulated licensed rights. End of! I'm sure my staff will tell you it's my leadership style – a sort of benign dictatorship, but with IP it is my experience that tells me joint ownership spells problems.

Try it at your peril is my advice. And, unless it is tightly controlled, you can fling caution to the wind if you jointly own the business IP with an overseas partner. Where IP is jointly owned, you can kiss goodbye to the control and commercialisation of it in many instances. Having an IP holding company* is one way around this. The short point is keep your IP in your business!

> *If you'd like to know more about IP holding companies in particular visit my blog at www.virtuosolegal.com where you'll also find detail on a whole range of IP related issues.

Step 3
Getting Protected

If you only read one chapter in this book then read this one! Yes, this one is a big fat important chapter.

If you have a squatter in your house, you take the title deeds to court, show the Judge that you own the house (because you have the deeds and are named on them). Then in most circumstances the court will grant you an order to have the squatters evicted. Everyone understands that. The broad principle is the same in IP. If you have a registered right such as a trade mark, a patent or a registered design right, then you can take your legal rights to court for enforcement. The route for enforcement of unregistered rights still applies but a bit like unregistered land rights. The boundaries of the property can be much more difficult to establish, especially where there are no agreed plans to show demarcation lines. If you don't think registration is important, then here is a quote from my client Brian Dickson, MD of Sport Direct Limited in the UK.

"We were so busy when we set up Sport Direct originally that we didn't register our trade mark Sport Direct for

our cycle accessory business straight away. In fact it was several months before we applied to get the mark registered. You can imagine our horror a few months later when another company started to use Sports Direct widely for selling a variety of sportswear and goods. It took us years and a great deal of money to finally get our mark recognised by the trade mark office. There has of course been widespread confusion of our two marks – often to our detriment."

So what can be protected? Let's have a look at the basics:

Why Patent?

Filing for a patent is complicated and not for the amateur. A patent can be granted on new technology, such as a new detergent or drug. Provided the formula is both new and there are new technical effects, the product and the process for making the detergent or drug can probably be protected.

Unless you patent your technology, then once it is in the public domain, pretty much anyone can use it without paying you a fee!

Why go to all the trouble of creating new technology and then let everyone use it for free? Some new technology may be free to start with – but there are often good reasons for giving it away at the start in order to get traction in the market.

What can be protected by a patent?

The essential criteria are that the product or process must be new, must be "capable of industrial application" and must not be obvious. The tests are not understandable to most people, but in broad terms you can't patent things such as new surgical techniques, although you could patent a new piece of surgical equipment. Software is specifically excluded from being patented, but again the law is not clear to the layman as certain software driven improvements may be patentable. In the USA software and business methods are patentable, so the regime in the USA is different. In some instances, it is worthwhile looking at patenting something just for use and protection in the USA.

Once a patent is filed, with a description of the technology there is a rigorous examination process and a patent can proceed to grant only once the examiner is satisfied that the technology is new and inventive. Patent filing strategies can be complex depending on the competition in that area.

Prior Art Searching – What Is It?

This is the term experts' use when looking at the existing registers of IP round the World. So for example big companies will routinely look at patent registers and applications for patents before embarking on research. There is no point in spending millions of pounds on R&D when someone has already applied for a patent which will knock out the area of technology for which you require cover. Having said that, where companies haven't been advised, it is certainly not an unknown thing for companies to do just that with their money. The same applies for trade marks and RDs. Well informed big multinational companies look long and hard at their global brands undertaking dozens of clearance searches before deciding on a new brand name. Again there is no point in creating a global brand without first of all checking you can use it where you require and also having a native speaker do searches for phonetically similar words or choosing brands that will just embarrass the brand owner in a particular country. I mean *Pschitt*® lemonade has never been exported to the UK from France! A few of my other favourite names are *Mukk*® yogurt in Italy, and the well-known German toilet paper *Happy End*®.

Prior art searches may seem expensive but they pay off in the long run. If you find out in advance that your registration will fail or will be challenged, not only will you find out who is doing what and where, you are highly likely to save filing and other fees. Searching is not foolproof – there is only so far that searches can go, but at least they do flag up the icebergs. Also bear in mind that professionals use very sophisticated databases to do their searches – these software programmes can cross reference dozens of potential conflicting very quickly. Do them manually and it will take ages and you are likely to miss lots of things.

Below I've set out the things to me which you should know and are business critical when considering patenting:

1. Always, always do a "prior art" search first. There is no point in submitting something for patenting when it is likely or

even possible that someone else has got there first. I've seen people who've not been advised of this often they waste their money filing because they meet obstacles in the examination process due to prior art which has been filed - by which time they've wasted thousands of pounds on filing the patent. I regularly assist clients with what is termed as "landscaping" the technology, i.e. looking to see what is already out there. Be strategic - a good report can save you thousands.

2. **Patenting is not cheap. Don't go into it expecting to pay a few hundred pounds.** The basic costs start at around £3000 and they go up from there depending on how widely you file, how many translations you have done and how much prior art searching you do. BUT do see it as an investment – without it your product can be copied by anyone.

3. **You do not generally need worldwide patent cover.** Bear in mind that patent attorneys, like lawyers, are often internally rewarded in their employment for doing more filing and drafting, so their advice can be distorted by what's in it for them. Also, many of them make a great deal of money from receiving incoming work from other overseas patent attorneys. That is NOT to say you don't need international cover. You do! However, there are strategic ways of getting what you need and what you can afford to protect.

4. **Select where you need cover and try and keep translation costs to a minimum.** Translation costs can soon mount up in an international patent filing. International patent filing is

often called a "PCT". It stands for Patent Cooperation Treaty and means you can use one filing point for many countries you want cover. Frankly speaking in some countries there is no point in patenting as your patent MAY take years to be granted and even then may not be enforceable.

5. **Always find a patent attorney who understands your technology.** Many patent attorneys have good scientific qualifications and many have PhD's. Find one that has an insight into what you're doing. He or she may not be the one you've used in the past.

6. **Patent attorneys outside London may have lower rates – as do solicitors.** In fact some very good patent attorneys (and solicitors) choose to live and work outside London for lifestyle reasons. Shop around. There are lists of suitably qualified people on the Chartered Institute of Patent Attorneys website. www.cipa.org.uk. HOWEVER, ALWAYS appoint the best person for the job – the right person MAY cost more but MAY also do a better job.

7. **Don't be tempted to draft a patent specification and claim yourself.** Drafting patents is a dark art and believe me, self drafted patents, even if granted, are often difficult to defend in infringement proceedings. They are also, generally speaking, of little interest to investors for a variety of reasons, including the fact that they're difficult to enforce. The UK for some reason excels itself in this strange practice. Around

20% of all patents filed in the UK are not filed by patent attorneys but by inventors; however, less than 2% of **granted** patents are filed by inventors. It doesn't take a genius to work out that it pays here to get the right advice – and pay for it or waste your time completely.

8. **Bear in mind that patenting isn't the be all and end all** and that sometimes, tactically and economically, other methods will work for you. Some industries keep things as trade secrets, some file for Registered Designs which are a fraction of the cost but don't protect the actual invention as such; and sometimes technology is so fast moving patenting can be a waste of time and money.

A few years ago I was invited onto a panel of speakers at a fantastic event organised by the European Patent Office (EPO). The event was held to celebrate new ideas and inventions. Simply attending it and finding out what was happening across the world in terms of ground breaking new technology was fascinating. On the panel I was joined by John Burt who at the time was the Head of Patents at IBM. He and I rather publicly locked horns in a debate about smaller businesses bringing their patents to IBM or other large companies for their perusal. John's strategy was to only entertain technology that had proceeded seamlessly and quickly through the patenting process. I pointed out to him that this was fine, but only provided those businesses which did take technology to him knew how to navigate the patenting system and had been properly advised. In fact we were both right in a way. John's point was that if something is quite new it can sail through to grant with little difficulty in as little as nine months, especially if expedited. If it does that, then the IBM's of this world are very interested in acquisition, as the technology is certainly cutting edge. However, my point was that many smaller businesses, without a team of patent attorneys and specialists advising them, just don't know and don't get advised as to this type of strategy and how it works, especially in the software industry. Sadly this means that some big businesses completely miss first class technology from smaller businesses. Where do you stand?

IP Accelerator Points

- **Consider whether or not your technology needs some kind of patent strategy behind it.** If you're in a competitive industry then a strategy and patent informatics (i.e. who is doing what) are very worthwhile. Also, if you are considering investment or a trade sale then see time investing in a strategy as being of value to the company. As so few companies complete a strategy in a thorough and meaningful way. If you can present a compelling story and informatics to an investor or a buyer then you're likely to knock their socks off and stand out from the crowd.

- **If you are a small business and you want to sell or licence your patents to a bigger company, find out what they already do patent-wise.** What areas are they looking at for new technology? What patent strategies have they got? Who is in charge of this review?

- **Always do prior art searching.** Unless your product or process is entirely new it is highly likely that someone else has something similar if not "knock out" in terms of prior art (i.e. prior art that effectively "knocks out" the provided disclosure). Used properly, prior art searching will help your patent attorney draft your specification and claims.

- **Don't think you can patent on the cheap!** If time isn't against you, then reserve the filing of your patent until such times as you can afford good professional advice. Make full use of none disclosure agreements to make sure you retain the right to patent. Telling everyone at the latest conference about your great ideas, whilst satisfying, is often the wrong thing to do if you haven't yet filed your patent! Your smug feeling will soon wear off if you find you've lost your commercial advantage by disclosing too early. The same applies when you publish in a scientific journal.

- **Get the right patent attorney,** file only where you need to, can afford and will be trading, and set out a roadmap of costs and timelines to meet your goals.

- **Think carefully about expensive overseas patent filing.** You may well want to cover your technology with a patent in China, as it is the only way of getting the Chinese to take action in China against infringers. However, the brutal fact is that patent cover in some countries is hardly worthwhile, as local courts will never stop infringers. Also, some countries will deliberately delay or deny examination and grant in some technological areas.

- **If you want to be a global business then create a global strategy early,** so that you can enter new markets with the right protection.

Trade Marks

Why Register?

There is an easy answer to this one – **registration of your brand in whatever format is the BEST and in some cases ONLY way of protecting the business reputation you create!**

Of all the things businesses get wrong, the key one is their trade mark as their brand. It is vital to get it right – getting it wrong is very expensive. A company name or domain name, whilst important, is actually only part of your brand – registration confers the ultimate protection.

What can be registered?

OK, which of the following do you think can be registered as trade marks?

A word

A logo

A jingle

Two dimensional shapes

A colour

A smell

The answer is all of them, and indeed combinations of the above! So, it is possible to register your trading name and your logo in say for example, a particular colour. Big brand owners also look at registering their slogans jingles and specific shapes. A quick look at the trade mark registry at www.ipo.gov.uk will show you just how widely trade marks can be used. By way of example, the shape of the *Polo Mint®* is registered as well as the brand name. However, the basic test is that the mark or brand – whatever it is, is distinctive but not descriptive of your goods and services. Brands which are descriptive are not capable of trade mark protection, so a mark such as "Leeds Printing Services" would not be registerable; however, a Leeds-based printing and scanning service called "Lodis" would be distinctive and could be registered as a trade mark.

The other issue to consider is whether or not the mark is capable of graphical representation. So for example, if you register a jingle you are registering the musical annotation of that jingle. Indeed the aural representation or sound of some marks is very important to the brand owners, think of the four notes that always accompany the *Intel®* TV advertising. Colours must be registered by reference to a particular pantone or similar precise colour reference. Having said that some colours are, of themselves, quite distinctive of certain products. Cadbury's purple chocolate wrapper and BP's distinctive green are great examples of iconic brand colours. *Little known fact: Some marketers use packaging colours to make consumers think of particular associations – blue packaging for water products or something "clean" such as bleach for example. It is quite common to find colours associated with certain food flavours – red for beef or salt flavours! The use of colours in advertising can be very powerful when it comes to catching a consumer's eye on the shelves of a supermarket. So do you need to register a colour on your trade mark to make it unique to you and therefore easily recognised.*

Logos as Trade Marks and Brands

Logos and graphics are also capable of being registered trade marks and some logos are well known brands. For example, the shell shape for *Shell*® petroleum and similar products is very distinctive and has huge value on its own. Everyone knows the shell logo and associates it with the company. One question I'm regularly asked is whether or not to do two separate registrations - one for a word mark and one for a logo mark or whether to do them as a combination. The quick answer is to consider how they will be used in any branding exercise. If they will always be used together then it may be possible to save costs and just file for one mark. Generally however, they are separately registered so that the different marks can be used on their own. So, if, for example, you are using the word mark only on the packaging but both logo and word mark on the swing tag, then you'd probably be better registering two marks.

A trade mark or brand has to be classified when an application is made for registration. By this I mean the use of the mark has to fall into one of 45 classes. If you wanted to register a trade mark for use on clothes you'd register the mark in class 25 and possibly class 24 for textiles, depending on how you will use the brand. My legal practice, Virtuoso Legal, is registered in class 45 for legal services; however, we still sometimes get the post for another unconnected business – Virtuoso Plastering! Luckily that doesn't confuse anyone of course and were they to register, the business would be another entirely separate class.

Why Registration of the Brand Trade Mark is so important?

First of all, registration of IP confers a monopoly of use. In my case Virtuoso Legal is exclusively our trading name. If anyone else wanted to use that mark for legal services I could ask the court to stop them from doing so.

Legal action with a registered trade mark is much easier than if your mark is not registered.

This is especially so overseas, where the laws of "passing off" (the tort or law concerning civil wrong doings as opposed to criminal wrong doings, that people use where they haven't got a registered mark but want to protect the goodwill they've accrued in a name) can be very variable and unsatisfactory. If you want to export it is vital that you get your trade mark registered both in the UK and elsewhere. If you don't then someone else probably will register the mark and you may well lose your opportunity in different markets. Within the UK we use the term "passing off", yet the equivalent type of court action overseas is often called trade dress, especially in the USA.

Another key reason is that should you wish to licence the mark out, by licensing or franchising a business concept for example, really needs a strong brand and a registered mark to be successful.

Registration of your brands as trade mark allows you to protect your market and enhances the value of your business.

Once you've created a brand by registering your trade mark, then you can create a "brand promise" that delivers the kind of products or services you want to associate with that brand. But bear in mind that to an IP lawyer, your brand and your trade mark are not necessarily one and the same. (I know – we lawyers are all very particular when it comes to language!)

Brands are used to position products and services in the minds of the consumer and they are of increasing importance in trade, especially overseas trade where people need to associate a brand with an expectation.

Many businesses these days go to extraordinary lengths to describe their brand values, especially where the brand is licensed. It is, for example, highly destructive to create a brand which promises excellent quality but overseas under the governance of a licensee, that brand value becomes meaningless. History is littered with examples of different brands having different values in different countries. This is a good way of actually devaluing the global position and value of a trade mark.

If you want to create a global brand you must make your

licensees understand and contractually comply with YOUR vision of the brand and not theirs! This means clear understanding of the brand values, backed up by contracts which place obligations on the licensee.

The trade mark is, if you like, the registered bit of the brand, so for my legal practice we have the name Virtuoso and the logo – a stylised VL. However, the brand is what we deliver as a whole entity, i.e. service, quality and true expertise. If we were a consumer brand we may have, as part of our brand proposition, fancy packaging, or delivery only through approved suppliers etc. At the end of the day your customers need to remember key points about your brand and that is usually a name and logo and what that promises to THEM.

What Happens with Unregistered Marks?

If your trade mark is not registered then it is much more difficult to stop other people coming along and using the same mark or something very like it in order to piggy back off your goodwill and trading representation. Especially in overseas markets. The problem is that even in the UK, whilst the laws of "passing off" are well established, procedurally it takes much more effort to prove your case. In the UK there is a "3 step" test for passing off. These are the elements the court looks at to establish your case:

1. Does your unregistered mark have any goodwill attached to it? In simple terms this means how much have you used it recently, where have you used it and for what purposes? How much have you spent on advertising it and how well known is it?

2. **Does the new mark misrepresent itself as or for your goods and services.** In other words is the other mark likely to confuse the public? Is it used on similar goods or on something quite different?

3. **Is the new mark likely to cause damage to the existing mark?** Does the new mark lead people into buying other peoples goods and services are a result of its use? If people buy someone else's goods rather than yours, then damage has and will continue to occur until stopped!

On a personal level I find this quite an easy concept to understand. The steps aren't confusing. You've used the mark, you've seen someone else with a similar mark and they have stolen your business. But, the courts normally ask for a whole raft of evidence about the above BEFORE they will grant an injunction and stop the other mark from being used. Putting together lots and lots of evidence equals lawyers spending hours and hours preparing it for the court and this usually means a great deal of cost.

So the choice is yours –spend a few hundred quid and protect your brand or watch someone else come in and steal your market, devalue what you're doing and pinch your customers.

It is often a 'no brainer' to register what you can, as early as you can. You can find a breakdown of current UK, European and US registration costs on my website at www.virtuosolegal.com . A registration is granted usually within a year and you then get 10 years from the filing date as cover. Be warned however, you must use your mark within five years of filing or it can be wiped off the register on the grounds of non-use.

IP Accelerator Points

- Look at what can and should be distinctive about your goods and services with a view to registering.

- Look at not only the market you're currently in but also at the markets and arenas you wish to move into. For example, will you move your cosmetics brand into beauty services such as salon treatments and do you need to add this category or "class" from the start to your application to save future filing fees? If so, it can be easier to add it at day one.

- Do you wish to trade globally? Then consider using trade mark filings under the Community Mark scheme (i.e. all members of the EU under one filing) and then globally for a "Madrid Protocol" filing. Ask a professional IP lawyer or trade mark attorney about using these steps, as they could save you a lot in filing costs.

- It is possible to file your own trade marks but a professional will save you time, money and potential heartache, especially if there is a global element to your current or future trade. Get it wrong and you automatically lose your filing fees and then you've saved nothing at all!

- Do proper clearance searches! These need to be done professionally using professional databases and local advice. There is no point in simply filing if there are identical or similar marks already filed or pending. All that will happen is that you will waste thousands in filing fees.

- Do not allow your mark to be shared by agents' distributors or collaborators without your guidance and control. In particular you should always <u>own</u> your trade marks outright. Don't be fooled into sharing ownership overseas!

Registered Design Rights – Why Bother?

Registered Design Rights (RDs) are often the Cinderella of IP rights. Usually overlooked, often ignored and underrated they often come into their own in terms of strategic IP value.

RDs are used to protect the "look" of something. By way of example, some toy manufacturers and car makers use RDs to protect a toy or car component that has "eye appeal". RDs cover a number of everyday items such as certain types of packaging through to decorative lamps, picture frames and medical devices.

If something is designed and created for its attractive looks, registration gives the product a much longer period of protection than simply relying on unregistered design rights.

Remember I talked earlier in the book about Apple's iPod as a good example; there were MP3 players on the market well before it, but the design of the iPod meant everyone wanted one. In a modern economy, RDs can be used to stop "knock off" copies flooding the market with cheap imitations.

RDs will last for 25 years provided the renewal fees are paid. Registration by way of two dimensional drawings is reasonably straight forward and applications are made to register a design in the UK through the Intellectual Property Office (IPO). The application must be new. Absolute novelty, as in never seen before type novelty used to be a requirement for registration but now UK law allows businesses to use, improve and develop the RD for up to a year before deciding whether or not to proceed with registration. This is known as "deferred registration" and allows the applicant a filing or "protection" date which may be up to a year before publication and the resulting exposure to scrutiny in the public domain. This one year period of grace has made using RDs much more popular than before, as it allows businesses to register popular designs AFTER they've proved popular.

An RD can used for the whole or parts of the design, so say, for example, the product had an attractive relief type pattern on it as well as attractive design features, then the surface decoration as well as the product's overall design could be eligible for registration.

As with all registered IP, the protection of registered designs is easier through the court system than the protection of unregistered ones. In simple terms the registered monopoly is far easier to protect.

My own feeling about RD is that it encourages businesses to look at and improve the attractiveness of everyday products. As for trade marks, it is now relatively easy and relatively inexpensive to get European cover for your RD and indeed that is what many smart companies do. A great example I looked at earlier in the book is Off the Wall Limited, a TV stand manufacturer in Bradford.

Off the Wall registered the "look" or design of their TV stands in order to deter copying or plagiarism. They invested in cutting edge attractive designs in a competitive market where price had become all important as all TV stands looked so similar. Companies that use RDs often have well informed management teams, and in a busy market place in my mind that is what makes them stand out from the crowd.

Strategically, RDs can be used in addition to the patenting process. If patenting fails for one reason or another, a business can fall back on its RD for protection of the "look" of their product.

IP Accelerator Points

- Does the product have significant new and attractive design features? If so consider registration of an RD.

- Are you designing a product which is likely to be copied by "me too" type competitors? If so an RD may provide valuable protection.

- Is the product likely to be sold because of its design alone or in spite of it – say for example where it bears a well-known trade mark and has a demand purely because of the brand?

Costs versus Benefits with Filing

This is a subject I'm quite keen on! As a business owner myself I like to know that my money is being wisely spent. I've seen quite a number of what I would term "vanity" filings; in other words filings that don't serve a commercial purpose but satisfy the applicant. By way of example, I once saw a patent filed for a complex and expensive toy in South Africa. There was no market out there for the toy but the inventor was originally South African and thousands of pounds were in my mind wasted on protection where the product was unlikely to sell and was easily ripped off with very little by way of protection from the courts. I've also seen businesses encouraged to file in countries where it is frankly a waste of time and effort. Having said all that it is usually better to have more registrations than fewer.

Patent and Trade Mark Attorneys don't know your business – you do!

It is also true to say that most of them have very little practical experience of court litigation and they are often, therefore, not well placed to comment on how easily court action can be commenced or even judgements enforced. It is not uncommon now to see Trade Mark and Patent Attorneys with litigation qualifications; however, few have much practical experience of litigation. There has to be good commercial reasons and strategies to litigate and that can be difficult for a novice to litigation to assess.

It is also well worthwhile discussing with your advisor the use of international protocols to save money on international filings. Best practice would be to decide up front where you want to sell products, where you want to make products and what will be your most lucrative markets. If you have a roadmap of this kind, you can then plan a timeline of filing and costs that will suit your business. Filing without a plan can waste your money and it isn't cheap to get cover in some countries. Additionally, unless you are already using a mark in some parts of the world, getting a registration in some countries such as the USA can be challenging.

Investors and Registered IP
- Enter TV's *Dragon's Den*

If you're a fan of the BBC TV programme *Dragon's Den* (and I must admit I have a love/hate relationship with it) then you'll know-how frequently the "Dragon" investors ask prospective businesses about their IP. I'm not entirely sure that the Dragons have a full understanding of IP, but make no mistake LOTS of investors do. Some of them have had businesses that have crashed and burned because their IP wasn't in order! A lesson they're unlikely to forget. In addition some of the big investment houses are highly likely to employ experts who will check out the IP before investing. Here's a true story about Fusion Nutraceuticals Limited (FNL) in Ireland.

At the time FNL was a relatively new company, although the management team did have a great deal of experience under their belt running other companies. The background to their product and their company is fascinating. FNL manufacture a product known as Sucralose. This extremely sweet substance was originally made from sugar cane and was discovered and refined by scientists at Tate &Lyle® some 25 years ago. The basic product was patented and Tate &Lyle cleverly created something of a patent thicket around the manufacturing process, as well as the product.

The beauty of Sucralose is that, not only is it an artificial sweetener without a horrible after taste, but it contains virtually no calories and is not denatured by heat. As such it can be used in many manufacturing processes to reduce the calorie content of food but keep the sweet taste. Given the vast increase worldwide in the number of type II diabetics, and the demand for sweet but low calorie products, the market potential was huge and growing. It also accounted for a considerable part of Tate &Lyles profits. A poor grade Sucralose product has being manufactured in China for a few years but the manufacturing process used was unreliable meaning the product quality varied, yields were low and the consumer experience was poor.

In 2008 FNL found a suitable manufacturing site in India and looked into making Sucralose, which by then had come off patent, as had some of the key manufacturing techniques. FNL invested heavily in patent clearance searching and also in engaging my services and those of specialist consultants in the commercialization of intellectual property and related technology Burgundy Gold Limited to look at fending off any attack from Tate &Lyle. It was only by "girding their loins" in such a defensive way that FNL managed to gain funding from external investors. Without looking extensively at the IP background in detail, FNL could have crashed and burned. Thanks to some skilful work and management it did not and the investors very much liked the strategic way that FNL had invested time and effort into making sure that every angle had been covered. FNL's Sucralose is now sold extensively in the UK and is set to be a huge international success.

Investors understand that registered IP is much easier to defend, much easier to commercialise and much easier to sell on. Now, have I convinced you this could be useful?

Step 4
The Enemy Within

Commonly called your staff or someone else's!

Staff are the major asset of any business. Without great staff you can't have a great business. I know this from personal experience; however, from time to time every business has a member of staff who turns out to be less than helpful and sometimes downright malicious. We're now going to look at how IP and staff issues overlap in a business.

Why Staff Contracts are Important

It is good practice to have staff and directors contracts that specifically cover IP issues. If someone is paid to invent or create, then don't expect that creativity to stop every evening as your staff member or director leaves the building to go home. Lots of people have their own creative areas at home – whether it is the home PC or a workshop. If they are likely to create IP in their own time at home, it may well be worthwhile covering this expressly in an employment contract. Senior people within the organisation can be the highest risk, as not only are they likely to have been founder members of the business, but they are often more than capable of making improvements and generally doing their own thing as a sideline if required. There can then be a blurring of lines, as to what is created for their work and what is created for themselves – or even in extreme cases a parallel business. (More of that one later, as it is hugely damaging when it arises.)

For the sake of clarity it is important to expressly state what someone is expected to create for the company and say that the business owns it, so that there can be no ambiguity..

Problems often arise with copyright material, as the first owner of copyright is the author him or herself (you'll find more on copyright specifically in Step 5 – Copyrights and Wrongs). Software contractors for example, may own the code that they create and it is important, therefore, to be clear that anything they do for you as a contactor or otherwise belongs to the business. Similar problems arise with directors – I've often found that senior staff just don't like the challenge of sorting out this issue with fellow directors. The best way round it is to make sure it is covered before any real disputes can occur. In simple terms this means early on in the lifecycle of the business - preferably at the start when there is no money or lucrative revenue streams in the business to argue over!

Get your employment contracts and shareholders agreements in place early and set out all the IP issues. It is FAR cheaper than sorting it out when you've fallen out after a year or two.

Access All Areas

The problem in some organisations is that some staff have access to everything on the IT system. And by that I mean everything that is useful and has a value. By way of example, things such as customer records, spending patterns, databases, design drawings and so on, may often be accessed by numerous people. Indeed that is the only way some companies can work. However, it is equally easy to install software systems that monitor staff activities. In that way, it is possible to monitor when someone downloads a whole database for example. I'm not suggesting for one minute that IT staff spend a lot of time on this, but at least with a tracker programme on the system major problems of this nature can at least be identified, monitored or and if necessary tackled. One of the biggest problems for companies is where there are redundancies or management practices which hack staff off. Unhappy staff members are always the biggest risk and sometimes they will wreck or delete a database just for the hell of it when leaving. Even worse can be taking it wholesale to a competitor!

There is another good reason for monitoring key material on your IT systems and that is to control access to certain reports or data that you don't want everyone to see. A classic example of this would be the need to keep research material drawings and designs in conditions of complete confidence. I've had several unhappy clients in front of me where their lead designer has left and emailed an entire portfolio of designs or database of customers to a home email, or where test results have been on a shared access computer where anyone could and has indeed copied them.

Bear in mind it has never been easier to copy something – whether it is by reverse engineering or by electronic means. To some staff this means the door to the safe containing the crown jewels is always open.

Provided it is not too invasive, it is perfectly easy to set up access controls on most systems and monitor staff.

Another easy and essential thing to do is to have an email policy for staff as part of your Terms and Conditions of Employment and make it clear what is or is not acceptable practice. Do beware though, overly invasive email monitoring has a number of downsides. In the worst case scenario it can land you in trouble with the data protection registrar or an employment tribunal. Also, nosey IT directors can be all too powerful in terms of seeing confidential information and can really upset staff with their attitude. You may be thinking of selling the company for example and the IT director may not be happy about working for another employer and spill the beans covertly to your staff. It has been known!

Non-disclosures and Trade Secrets

Companies often use non-disclosure agreements (NDA) to provide information to third parties under obligations of confidence. This may arise for example where technology hasn't been perfected, or where a patent application is to be filed. NDA's are also used where financial and other restricted information is going out. NDAs are covered further later in the book. However, where critical data is to be disclosed it is good practice to know how the other side will distribute the information. Who will it be disclosed to – is there a list of individuals? Mark the actual information as **confidential** and also as **copyright** © and make sure everyone knows its source, its ownership and to whom it is to be presented and for what purpose.

There is often some kind of reciprocal terms in NDAs. Simply put – "we'll show you our trade secrets, you show us yours and we shall see if we can do business together." In the main trade secrets should only be shared for short periods of time for evaluation purposes. It isn't good practice to leave them open-ended time wise, and it is good practice to make sure all copies of documents are destroyed or handed back once the period of evaluation is closed.

Problems often arise where small companies make disclosures to bigger companies. In large drug companies, for example, with varied R&D programmes, there may be dozens of different research departments and trade secrets can be disclosed accidently or deliberately to people who are involved on similar projects to the business who submitted the work. The only way to guard against this is to set out the scope of the disclosure from the start.

Restrictive Covenants and Confidential Information

Restrictive covenants are obligations on the employee not to do certain things after they've left. You will also find them in business sale contracts, e.g. not to open a competitor shop within so many miles of the first successful one you've sold. The useful thing is that they concentrate everyone's mind on what is of use in the company. It is not unusual for the standard employment contract to state whether or not it is possible to solicit customers or suppliers or even staff after the employee has left.

As a rule of thumb most restriction covenants in an employment contract can only last six months or so and you'll find that the courts won't uphold terms where the employee is bound to keep them for much longer. The rules surrounding confidential information, however, are different.

Confidential Information Must Remain Secret and not be Used or Disclosed by a Former Employee.

The debate that often arises here is "what is confidential", as so called confidential information from a client's point of view is often not what the law understands it to be. Obligations of confidentiality are also implied within employees' contracts – they don't have to be expressly stated, but it is clearer if they are.

Again, the ease with which staff can copy material from a company's computer systems comes into play. One of my particular areas of interest and expertise relates to identifying and obtaining the evidence for where copying has occurred.

A strong word of caution here… If you suspect that an employee has taken or downloaded material from your company computer systems do not let your IT staff, however experienced, investigate.

For evidence to be gathered and used in a proper forensic fashion you need to seek expert advice, especially where you suspect criminal conduct such as theft or fraud. You are only going to get one crack at getting this right and if the lawyers and IT people who do the investigation get it wrong then your case may fall apart. Your inclination may be to involve the police from the start, and certainly in some circumstances this is the right thing to do, for example where several people and external associates appear to be involved. However, the sad fact of the matter is that if you do involve the police, as criminal acts may have occurred, you can expect to sit around a great deal and loose quite a lot of valuable work time whilst they investigate your business. The police may also ultimately drop charges as crimes of this type are so time consuming and demanding of their very limited resources in this area. When this happens you are left to use civil remedies against former staff, which is time consuming and expensive.

What Happens When it all Goes Wrong?

Luckily the instances of current or former employees causing real havoc are few and far between; however, when they do, the damage can be catastrophic and irrevocable. The remedies available to employers are wide ranging and draconian. They include civil "search orders": searching premises and computers, "freezing orders": where the individual's bank accounts are frozen and injunctions: orders which prevent something from happening. I've been on all sides of these arguments and I am an experienced "supervising solicitor". This means I am entrusted by the claimants and the courts in serving court orders, such as search orders, and then overseeing the actual search. Often advising the claimant's solicitors on how to do the IT forensics. I work closely with an organisation called MD5 who specialise in telephone and IT forensics and am grateful to them for providing me with such in-depth knowledge of what is or isn't possible technically. All former police trained, few organisations know how to obtain the forensic clones of IT systems as well as MD5 and I really value the standard of work they produce in this challenging area – not everyone works to such standards.

Highly complex and in depth, the subject of IT forensics is a book in itself and the law in this area is constantly changing. The key to all of it is preparation and be prepared for a fairly large legal bill at the end of it. In relative terms, however, this may be a small price to pay for getting rid of staff that have done hundreds of thousands of pounds worth of damage to the company. It may also be a way of recovering money which has been dishonestly obtained and rectifying a very major wrong.

What should employers do if they suspect things are going wrong?

First and foremost investigate all suspicions promptly, thoroughly and obtain the evidence you need before alerting the employee in question to your investigation.

It is important to preserve evidence in the right format. For example, every time you open an electronic document you leave a "finger print" on that document, showing the time and date it was opened and often by whom. It is, therefore, easy to see how possible evidence of wrong doing can be incorrectly attributed by someone who knows the IT system and how evidence might be tampered with by someone unawares. It is the IT equivalent of not using gloves to obtain forensic DNA evidence at the scene of a crime.

The evidence you require can be stored on servers, PC hard drives and mobile devices such as iPhones, iPads and Blackberrys. The list is endless. IT savvy employees are also increasingly using cloud or Internet based file hosting systems to upload information or email it out using Hotmail type accounts. The only foolproof way of storing evidence is to make a forensic clone of the original using specialised software. It is then possible to review a facsimile copy of the information taken.

The flip side to this is, of course, that employees have rights of privacy and it is a fine line between reviewing someone's IT activity because you feel you have legitimate grounds on which to do so and snooping into their private life on a hunch.

If you have noticed something is wrong, others will have done too.

There are often indicators that all is not well with some individuals who are up to no good and other staff may notice changes in a particular person's behaviour. For example, fellow staff may have noticed someone complain about work matters. They may not have had a promotion, a bonus or pay rise they were expecting. There could be problems at home with a partner in debt or a relative in trouble. A salesman could appear to be living well beyond their means. A financial controller may be reluctant to take holidays, or be overly protective and secretive about their work practices. It is easy to look back and recognise the signs once the damage is done yet even easier to write off strange behaviour because we don't like to believe that someone is being dishonest.

Once you've found out that there definitely is untoward activity going on you can take action. This may include putting the main suspect on "garden leave" whilst you investigate. This term is often used to describe a period of time when the employee is not required to be in work but is still being paid prior to dismissal or redundancy. You may dismiss them and contact your customer or supplier database to see if they are aware of what was happening. The important point is to DO SOMETHING. You'd be surprised how easily some staff can wipe out the value of a whole company in a relatively short space of time. Nobody is saying it is pleasant; I've never yet met a client who enjoyed this kind of investigation within their business, but, if nothing is done it is akin to letting your staff steal the goods from the shop floor, while you ignore them and you wouldn't do that would you?!

Step 5
Copyrights and Wrongs

Of all the areas of intellectual property, copyright is the most complex, misunderstood and technically challenged by the digital age.

Copyright material in the form of text, software, databases, drawings and websites now contribute millions to the value of businesses in the UK. Yet, it has never been easier to copy a design or text, and it has never been easier to manipulate and change a copyright work with very little effort. It is therefore vitally important to any UK business to have the copyright it owns, in apple pie, or, as I've mentioned before, good, systematic order.

In the UK the law is now littered with statutes trying to keep up with the many technical issues the digital age has thrown up. The last 10 years have seen ever increasing copyright legislation arrive on the statute books including; The Copyright and Rights in Databases

Regulations 1997, The Broadcasting Act 1996, Communications Act 2003, Electronic Communications Act 2000 Computer Misuse Act 1990 and the Digital Economy Act 2010 to name but a few. Frankly, it is difficult for most IP practioners to keep up, goodness knows how the general public are supposed to understand the detail of the legislation and urban myths abound, especially in relation to the Internet. Indeed, of all the telephone inquiries I get, copyright has to be the most common topic. The two fundamental points most business people miss are:

1. **All copyright material is owned by someone** – even if it is not marked as such.

2. **Even if you've paid someone to produce copyright material for you, such as text, photographs, drawing and software, you do not necessarily own that material.** In fact, in the absence of a contract to assign the rights to you from a third party then all you have is permission to use it via a licence – express or implied.

There is of course very little accurate and up to date information available on the Internet and even people who work with copyright on a day-to-day basis often don't have a firm grip on the detail and exceptions as to what is or isn't protected. Many non-specialist lawyers get it wrong and unregistered designs, which overlap with copyright legislation and cover functional designs is a confusing area for everyone – even the experts argue. It is a changing landscape and yet copyright is vital to many businesses. In some cases copyright material in the form of software or databases or written material represents the entire value of the company.

Important things to know about copyright in your busines

There is no registration process with copyright material in Europe, so as with all IP, audit trails of creation are key to the pursuit or defence of copying in copyright infringement. There are several companies who've sprung up on the Internet offering copyright validation / registration processes. It is not necessary to use them to prove you own a particular piece of copyright material. With employees employed to create copyright material, it is always good practice to have ownership rights vested in the employer by way of an employment contract. This minimises ownership disputes. First of all let's look at the historical basis of copyright in the UK.

In 1476 William Caxton introduced the printing press to England and he is widely credited with standardising the English language. Partnering with this ground breaking technological revolution was the astonishing ability to mass-produce things which, previously, had only been made by a few skilled craftsmen, namely books and printed matter. At the time the Church, of course, had something of a stranglehold on literacy and few common people had knowledge of anything other than the Bible as a written text. Prior to the invention of printing presses, teams of monks would sit and painstakingly handwrite the text, creating beautifully decorated manuscript copies of the Bible. The Church also kept other important records, particularly of commercial transactions, including land transfers, wills, legacies, land ownership and tenancies. Legal documents such as mortgages or indentures and conveyances were also all manually documented on parchment and bound by hand. With the advent of printing presses authorship would take on a far greater significance.

Copyright now covers everything from broadcasts to designs, literary works, sculpture, paintings, software and music. The

Copyright Designs and Patents Act 1988, together with its various amendments, forms the backbone of how rights arise and are dealt with. Copyright arises as soon as something is created and put into a permanent format. So, a recording of music for example has a copyright arising in the recording. If the music is then formatted into a score a second written copyright arises. Quite often copyright material is compounded together. Take for example "user generated content" on YouTube. In any one clip there could be copyrighted music, copyrighted script and copyrighted artwork and of course there is copyright in the actual production and editing of the clip itself. It is therefore easy to see how people can be caught out using material and effectively broadcasting it without the original copyright owner's permission. The same happens with music mash ups, where several artists and songs are mixed together to create a completely new copyright. There can, therefore, often be numerous layers to any one copyright product. A further example would be an anthology of poems – copyright arises individually in each work and collectively in the assembly.

For practical and commercial business purposes, copyright is often chopped down into royalty earning streams. For example, a photographer may allow his material only to be used in one form of advertising – use on a website but not for print. Further royalties being paid for print use. The same happens with TV programmes. A much higher royalty is paid for screening material for the first time than for repeating the production a few years later, or in repeat broadcasts. A series which is put onto a DVD will earn different royalties altogether from general broadcast rights. Databases of addresses may be bought – but used only once. It's worth knowing that such databases are seeded with information or "leads" which report back to the database owner when the licensed usage is exceeded.

Each industry has its norms as to what is or isn't acceptable in any given situation. A famous person may only allow their copyright image to be used for advertising and product endorsement upon payment, and photographers and professional broadcasters usually obtain legally termed "release rights" from people who are filmed or used as models commercially. Of course where celebrities are "papped" on their way out of a nightclub, no such release rights are signed or required to print the photographs. Unlike some countries with different privacy laws the UK permits these photographs to be used as desired by the photographer. It was for this reason that Prince William and his wife the Duchess of Cambridge used the French Courts to obtain an injunction to stop further publication of photographs taken of them during a private holiday in France. I have a very personal view on this, which is that intrusive photographs of this kind should be subject to laws of privacy in the UK too.

The island of Guernsey has also recently produced legislation that will allow "image rights" or copyright material of someone's "look" to be registered for protection. For some famous personalities I can see them heading off to Guernsey to register their image, so that they customise licenses and royalty streams from such registration. Already an off shore tax haven, this is a smart move for Guernsey, and is likely to be copied elsewhere.

Different copyright royalties could also be paid on different types of copyright work. Take a Harry Potter novel for example. JK Rowling could expect a stream of income from the book, another royalty from the film rights, a third from merchandising rights, a fourth from a theatre production and so on. This is often the way that businesses diversify into other arenas. Jamie Oliver probably makes more money from his books, his TV appearances and his endorsement of cookware than from his restaurants. This type of syndication is VERY important for certain businesses – and it's wise to make yourself aware of what licensing copyright material can do for your business.

One of the major disputes that occurs and leads to inquiries in my practice is the unauthorised use of images and other copyright material on the Internet. The problem here is that the general public are often blissfully unaware of these rights until the rights owners catch up with them. Images which appear for example on Google Images or elsewhere often do not have a copyright watermark on them but do in fact belong to someone.

Years ago when I started in the law, and before the Internet was freely available, I used to get clients call me where particularly useful or valuable photographs that belonged to them had found their way into an image library. Newspapers and other periodicals would then use such images, especially in selling advertising to local companies without paying the photographer or owner of the image. The situation now routinely arises on the Internet. Getty Images, a large, well known online photo library, regularly discover the illegal use of their copyright images throughout the Internet. To combat this wholesale infringement photo libraries like Getty now use software which trawls the Internet for illegally used photographs. They then make demands for payment from the website owner for the use of the image. From my experience such demands are way beyond that which the photo library would legitimately obtain from licensing the images through their official websites in the first place.

As you can imagine, the owners of music rights are very keen to pursue individuals who 'file share' music- peculiar to our internet age, this involves people downloading and copying music from websites that they haven't paid for, thus depriving the creators and producers of royalty income. Pursuit is often made by rights owners for lost royalties; however, this is a difficult area. Music rights holders have lobbied legislators for legislation that would compel internet service providers (ISPs) to disclose the end users or file sharers who download this kind of data. *By way of background, downloading such copyright material demands large amounts of digital data and, therefore, heavy data users are often (but not always) file sharers. In this way knowing who are big the data consumers is one way to discover* who is illegally downloading films and music. So far, it would seem, legislators have been reluctant to pursue this avenue and ISPs appear to be unwilling to disclose which of their customers may be infringing copyright simply by being heavy data consumers. The whole area is fraught with legal difficulty and technicalities. In short, unless payments are being made and taken for illegally shared files, the evidence is difficult (but not impossible) to obtain.

The main arguments (correctly in my view) are that if music and films were made relatively inexpensive to download, then, by and large, they would be paid for by the vast majority of people. The key commercial point is, in fact, that the main costs of the rights holders' lie in the making, producing and promoting of the copyright material – not in its distribution. Monitoring distribution is, however, the key to the return on the original investment.

Whatever your view, the Internet has changed the game forever.

The same thorny issues apply to books too. Printing is only a modest part of the cost of producing a book and for electronic printing the costs are even less.

As writers know only too well, it is the time and the know-how delivered through the content of any book that counts. That is where its real value lies.

Databases

An important and valuable tool in most companies is their supplier and customer databases. Today, companies often use sophisticated customer relationship management programs (CRMs) which can tell them who are their most important customers or cost effective suppliers. Hence databases can be extraordinarily valuable to businesses. Some industries, such as the telecoms and betting industries, with their reliance on vast complex data attach huge value to the databases they create. Indeed the first significant court case involving databases arose between the British Horse Racing Board (BHB), which we mentioned earlier in the book, and the high street gambling business Ladbrokes.

BHB kept and still keeps detailed information on all race horses, their riders, trainers, colours, and races in a vast database. They then licensed that information out to a whole range of people for the purposes of calculating odds and therefore predicting racing form, taking bets and running race meetings. The actual facts contained in the database were not confidential, nor, individually, were they of great interest; however, as a composite work and modelled in a particular way, the database had great use and value. There are thousands of databases of this kind – often used by big businesses to make the right call, from building stores in the right location to targeting customers for particular products.

Rights in databases arise once the material is collected and arranged by someone. There is always a skill and effort in such an arrangement and the courts are willing to protect the databases as a type of "lower" form of copyright. Prior to the legislation in this area it was quite difficult to protect databases, as they sometimes didn't qualify as being protectable as copyright works in themselves.

How long does copyright last?

Copyright in works of art and written copyright lasts for the life of the author plus 70 years. So, most copyright work is protected for a very long period. The duration of copyright in works including broadcast rights, recording rights, unregistered design rights and database rights, however, is of a much shorter time period. The first thing any copyright lawyer will check is the duration of such rights. There are also legislative provisions for international enforcement of such rights under something known as the Berne Convention. This useful treaty allows copyright material to be widely protected worldwide.

Collecting an income, also known as licensing

Income streams on copyright material may be acquired in different ways. It may come straight from licensing deals – owner to licensee. Alternatively, some industries such as newspapers, software and music owners use "collecting agencies" to recover an income and to enforce the proper use and licensing of their products. In the UK the Federation against Software Theft – or FAST as it is commonly known, police and closely monitor counterfeit and fake software being sold. FAST also acts on behalf of a number of key software producers and have sophisticated ways of monitoring who is selling what and how many copies a business should have of any particular type of software.

The Federation against Copyright Theft or FACT routinely monitor the distribution and sale of counterfeit films and music. The problem that both organisations face is that some people simply don't believe it is wrong to copy something and sell it commercially without making a royalty payment back to the original copyright owner. This dismissive or 'pirate' attitude deprives the copyright owner of money they have legitimately earned through their hard work and effort. Ultimately, without an income stream it is easy to understand how creative innovation dries up. A further issue arises as a great deal of counterfeit copyright goods are actually made and sold by organised criminal gangs and I look at this a little later in the book.

Collecting agencies also collect money on behalf of the big music rights owners. The Performing Rights Society, or PRS, for example, collects money for rights holders where music is used for public performances. This means that music in a pub and broadcast over public systems must all be licensed and this includes playing a radio at work. The royalties are collected in and then divided up between the artists according to popularity and how frequently tracks are played. Collecting agencies exist for various copyright owners. In actual fact it is the only way some copyright owners can ever hope to get paid for their material.

I sometimes get calls from clients who've had a visit or a letter from a collecting agency such as FAST or FACT. Clients doubt their existence or entitlement. It is my experience that few of these letters are scams and that in fact the collecting agency has already done their homework on a business BEFORE they get in touch. Believe me, collecting agencies DO exist and DO monitor use and licensing. They also normally have a fixed tariff fee and it is often difficult to move away from the fees they suggest. I'm not saying that they are fair – I am saying that as a business who uses licensed software and likes to listen to music (amongst many other copyright materials) you need to be aware of them!

In addition, some organisations such as FAST and FACT have and use draconian powers of search and seizure. They also take out private criminal prosecutions to obtain the best result for their copyright holders. The same applies to Trading Standards in the UK who occasionally police copyright theft. Most of their work relates to mass copying of copyright material such as films and music DVDs but they will also investigate companies who infringe any of their copyright members' rights generally. Again, the game changer here is the Internet. And piracy is rife!

Unregistered and Registered Design Rights

Unregistered design rights (UDR) are a branch of copyright. UDRs cover the industrial design of everyday items, such as newly designed components for a machine or domestic items. So, for example, if you design a new oil drum or beer keg, then design rights will arise in the item. In the UK the actual duration of the right is relatively short, and the absolute monopoly is only five years from the date of commercialisation. This means that after something has been on the market for five years, it can be copied but the copied objects must be licensed and a royalty must be paid to the owner of the design right. This is a type of compulsory licence arrangement which the courts will enforce. Many companies now consider using Registered Design Rights (RDRs) where there is an "eye appeal" to the design. So toys, car accessories and other objects are regularly the subject of RDRs in order to give them more protection from copying and higher commercial value generally, as they can be protected for up to 25 years.

It is not uncommon for companies to use RDRs in conjunction with other rights, such as trade marking and patenting to create a portfolio of protectable rights. RDRs are easy to apply for and unlike patenting the registration process is not vigorously examined by examiners looking for prior art.

The value of UDRs is regularly overlooked. It is my view that companies who regularly innovate their designs should look to protect their design investment. The UK is a nation of inventors, doers and creators and UDRs created by engineers, designers and inventors in this country should be valued and protected. There is also a European unregistered design right which will give protection to designs created anywhere in Europe. There is precious little case law in this area in respect of what is or isn't a copy, but the best test I find is the "duck test": –if it walks, quacks and looks like a duck then it is most probably a duck! Crude but basically true. **The test for copying is a visual one and it tends to be somewhat subjective and difficult for the business man to understand. In many cases, it isn't that easy for a Judge to decide either.**

Step 6
Licensing and Franchising

Sharing a good business model and more importantly – making money from it.

Whilst IP rights are all about monopolies, the most powerful and valuable aspect of creating them is sharing them with others for everyone's benefit. You don't have to look far to see how this business model works so well – Disney, Microsoft, the BBC, Ford, and Siemens to name but a few have built very profitable businesses on sharing goods, formats, products and services that they have developed to other businesses – even competitors. **Licensing creates valuable income streams to hundreds of businesses.**

History is also littered with stories of how people tried and failed to keep hold of a monopoly – remember our Venetian glass making apprentices? One of those apprentice glass blowers did eventually escape and, of course, spread the secret of making the highly coveted glass. The inventor of the Tetrapak® was eventually forced to licence the technology so that others could share its benefits. Compulsory licensing is rare but does arise from time to time – especially if technology is used in an anti-competitive way or is needed by Governments. Sir Frank Whittle was compelled to sell his jet engine technology to the British Government for the Second World War effort, although it has to be said he was not entirely happy to do so even if they did pay him a very modest amount for the invention.

If you've created something of value, then look at sharing it to make more profit!

The public are often aware of software licenses yet in the UK we don't use the copyright licensing model nearly enough and in some countries in the World they just don't understand it at all. Although the statistics are unreliable, as many licences are not generally formally documented and recorded at any one registry, in the USA there are around five times more licensing deals done than in the UK. The concept is simple and it has parallels in land law. First you build the house, then you lease out each of the rooms and take a rent from the tenants. The IP is the house, the tenants are licensees and the rent is a royalty. The difference is that IP is not bricks and mortar – it is something less tangible and that is where the misunderstandings often arise in licensing. **You can call making money from IP, by virtue of franchising, master licenses, syndicating, non exclusive licensing or leasing but as far as any legal specialist is concerned it is all licensing your IP. This is akin to 'sweating' any assets your company owns. If you want to make money out of it, make it work 24 hours a day, seven days a week.**

I always use the word licensing. To me licensing means carving up the IP to create revenue streams. Another term frequently used is franchising. This means different things to different people and my view is that it works better in some countries than others. **In the UK** franchising often doesn't have a good reputation for the simple reason that the profits made by franchisees are not as rosy as suggested by the franchisor. Returns on investment can be slow and can be beyond the franchisee / licensees control as the franchisor/ licensor struggles to find new business, expand their brand awareness and invest in value for the company as a whole. Some franchisors / licensors also franchise / licence too many businesses in one geographic area, leading to problems for the franchisees/ licensees competing for a diminishing market in one location. Finally, as a word of warning, some franchisees / licensees are compelled to buy goods at over inflated prices from the franchisor / licensor in the name of providing a consistent product. If you are looking at being the licensee I suppose the name of the game is beware of the small print and look carefully at what CAN be achieved in your geographic area.

Having said all that about franchising / licensing, **if properly formulated it can work very well indeed and I'm a big fan of using licensing as a vehicle for sharing the business with others.** The wonderful thing about licensing lies in its flexibility. Licensing permits a business to enter new markets and obtain market share. It also creates lots of new business opportunities. As the German economic model shows, lots of small businesses can underpin a successful national economy. (In case you hadn't noticed I run a business and I do think SMEs in particular are undervalued in the UK, but don't let me get on my soap box!).

The key requirements for successful licensing are:

1. You need an established, tried and tested business model, rich with protectable IP such as key brands, trade marks, expertise and know-how to hook customers in.

2. Find the right licensee. In real terms this means finding someone with a similar business ethos, interest and drive.

3. Ensure both parties operate on fair and reasonably flexible terms. **There is no point in licensing unless both parties are going to make a profitable return.** Some people do licence

on unfair terms. After a while it usually fails. There is little point in using terms that tie another party into something which doesn't work for them. It simply leads to empty coffers and a great deal of heartache, especially for the licensee.

If you are looking at licensing your products and services then invest in the right legal and accounting advice. You MUST get the framework right. Some businesses just licence the name or brand, others go into much more detail about the types of products and services they offer under that brand name. It is important to ensure that certain standards are met. By way of example, if you are using your name you will want to make sure that the goods offered under that name meet the established brand standards and customer expectation. Companies like Kellogs® will openly tell you that they only make and sell under their own brand. Carlsberg® on the other hand will tell you that their goods are made under licence. This means that the owners of the Carlsberg name Carlsberg A/S of Denmark will be particularly prescriptive about how their lager is brewed, packaged and sold. In simple terms they will direct every licensee about specific technical requirements in the manufacturing process but they don't make it all themselves. If you take a licence in a fast food restaurant chain you'll be told exactly how to dress your staff, lay out your premises, cook and sell your food.

Before embarking on licensing have in mind a clear set of objectives:

1. What is it that your licensees are going to make and sell?

2. How will they do so?

3. What time frame will you want them to get up and running in?

4. What geographic restrictions will you put on your licensees – for example will you permit another licensee within a certain geographical radius.

5. Are you going to set up a Master License in an overseas market and then let THEM find further licensees?

6. Will there be minimum sales targets?

7. How will you monitor what they do?

8. Who will undertake advertising, trade sales events, training?

9. What will be the upfront royalty payment and the on-going licence fees?

As you'll see there is a lot to think about. We routinely use checklists to go through these issues with clients. It isn't fool proof but it does help focus people on what is possible.

Licensing: A few variations and why they can be important

There are a few more things which you should know about licensing. Firstly, there are different types of licensing. **Exclusive licenses** mean that there is only **one** business allowed to supply or use goods and/ or services. A **sole licence** means that the **licensor and licensee** can operate together to provide goods and or services. A **non exclusive licence** means there can be a variable number of licensees, so dozens of businesses can use the IP.

A licence can be granted to operate in a particular location – the whole of Scotland for example. Frequency of royalty payments can be important too. In some businesses it is impossible to calculate sales until the end of the financial year. In others, monthly figures may be available. Obviously frequency of payment of royalty can dramatically affect cash flow and profit, so it is important to be clear. I well remember one licensee who didn't realise the major impact of the % royalties that he had to pay the licensor until the end of the first years trading – and when the licensor demanded payment, the licensee had to fold the business as the royalties destroyed the cash flow.

Minimum sales and termination provisions are vital too. If it isn't working then in my experience it is always better for both parties to be able to exit swiftly and cleanly. There may be very little that can be done to salvage a particular situation and it is better to have the exit provisions clearly stated before any dispute arises, as to the performance of either party to make something work. Litigation or disputes can be pointless and time consuming – avoid them if you can by using well drafted agreements and thinking things through before signing up.

The duration of the licence must also allow the parties to recoup the investment but not be strung along in an agreement that isn't working for years and years. Tied in with these provisions may be training. If goods or services aren't selling, especially overseas, then you may want to look at what it is that is slowing the sales down. Is it staff knowledge, or do customers have different expectations? If you set up overseas, make time to explore and train on how it can work locally, as well as back home. I recall Gerald Ratner of Ratner's jewellery setting up shops in Holland, only to find the Christmas markets very limited. Even the big players make mistakes.

There is also an opportunity to licence some unusual parts of the business. By this I mean databases and know-how may be licensed individually. This could be done where the licensee is using their own "front end" or name to the business. This is often known as **white labelling**. It is common in the software industry where behind the scenes platform technology is licensed to multiple parties, so that the back end of the software works in the same way but the customer facing website or online portal bears different business' names and logos or trading identities.

International licensing – why it is very important to look at this to make profit from overseas

Licensing comes into its own when looking at exporting. It is often much better to have a locally established business making and/ or selling your goods and services than setting up a new company in a country where you are not familiar with the markets, the local customs or the local laws. **Licensing is quite categorically NOT a joint venture** – it should be done on a commercial arm's length basis. A joint venture or JV implies the formation of a company in which both parties have a stake. There are major handicaps to this in international trade, as quite often businesses find themselves making decisions in which they have no interest or requirement to become involved with. For example, a JV may require joint decisions over all spending or taking on key staff. It is far better to have this at arms-length and let the local person on the ground make those decisions. If you don't trust them then they shouldn't be your licensee either!

We do an increasing number of these types of international licensing arrangements and we often encourage clients to use these as a vehicle for overseas trade, and increasing profit as they are flexible and usually work well for both parties. The contracts themselves may or may not be complex but it is very important to have the key issues covered such as what is the subject of the licence, what are the marketing proposals, when will royalties be paid and so on.

Key International Licensing Terms

1. What IP is being licensed – trade mark, product, know-how, recipe, patent, software, technology?
2. What is the scope of the license? All goods or just some of them etc.?
3. Royalty payments - when will they be paid? How will they be calculated? How does the licensee audit them?
4. What about local websites and marketing?
5. Will the licensor provide assistance to get the business off the ground and if so, how?
6. What will terminate the licence – minimum sales?
7. If it doesn't work out, how will both parties walk away and what are the run off provisions?

Many businesses use a **Master Licence** arrangement overseas. This gives a master licence to a business in a large geographic area with an opportunity to sub-licence to a multitude of smaller businesses. It works well, especially in places such as the USA where the Master Licensee can manufacture and find sub-licensees in each different state. Do be aware, however, that even if your governing contract law is English you will often need to take local legal advice on these types of arrangement and budget accordingly.

The Laws of England and Wales and why it is important to do business on YOUR terms

Any agreement we advise on is always covered by the laws of England and Wales. As a firm we're all qualified to do that; however, in any event the UK has been a trading nation for hundreds of years and we have an internationally recognised legal system with specialist lawyers and judges. We're seen to be a fair system internationally and we certainly are. With that in mind, overseas parties to an agreement have little to fear when it comes to courts and lawyers resolving disputes. The same can't be said in other countries. We strongly advise clients to use England and Wales as governing law as there is no prejudice to either party to the contract in the event of a dispute. If you do use another governing law then you are going to have to pay for locally qualified lawyers to review it.

Just as an aside, the laws of England and Wales are routinely used by parties who have no connection to the UK – they've simply chosen the UK as a fair and unbiased system. It is therefore common for the laws of England and Wales to be applied to shipping and insurance contracts even though the parties are around the World

A further word of caution here with some agreements – they can be caught by local laws whatever you do. For example, agency agreements may go onto a local trading register and therefore automatically be covered by local courts when it comes to disputes. As far as I'm aware this doesn't happen in most of the world but I'd be interested to hear from you if this has happened to you or someone you know. I knew of one large client of ours who's international business became caught up in one of these local registers in the

Middle East and the dispute with the local agent took years to resolve. I hope things are different now.

I would always advise you to always make sure your licence arrangements are expressly covered by the laws of England and Wales – that way if things do go wrong, you're deciding the issue on your own doorstep and you can avoid the cost and complication of overseas courts and slow and expensive legal systems.

Arbitration

Another common clause we see is an international arbitration clause. Arbitration is not court it is a direction given to both parties in a dispute by a suitably qualified expert. Whilst businesses that decide to have arbitration and sign up to say they will be bound by it, it isn't always binding upon the parties in quite the same way as a Court Order. It is also my view that sometimes it isn't any cheaper than litigation. Given that England and Wales have a good court system which by and large works reasonably well I can't see a problem with using it. Parties normally use lawyers to prepare for arbitration and the procedures are somewhat similar to court, so I can't see very much advantage in using arbitration in IP disputes. The exception to this may be big international IP disputes.

In any event the courts in England and Wales always encourage mediation as the first point of resolving disputes. Mediation is an excellent way of trying to bring the parties together to find their own commercial solution. Certainly for smaller disputes it can work very well indeed. It also permits the parties to air some "non-legal" issues that have caused smouldering resentment.

Overseas: Local laws and IP

Any IP that is registered locally may be the subject of local resolution when it comes to disputes. For example if a trade mark is jointly owned, or even worse owned by a licensee or distributor overseas, then a local court will decide how this is dealt with. The same applies to all registered rights. It isn't uncommon, therefore, to have a contract covered by the laws of England and Wales – and the dispute determined in the UK whilst a dispute over ownership is covered by a local court. Costly and complex!

Step 7
More Ways to Make Money

Routes to market. Or how to make much more money by exporting

It seems logical to me to follow a step solely on licensing with an overview of other routes to market. Surprise, surprise – there are lots! Once all your IP is in order you may need to consider a number of ways of getting your products and services to market. I have already touched on licensing and I intend to come back to it, as it is such a big subject. However, what follows is a gallop through other contractual scenarios that you may find useful.

Distribution Agreements

A very common way to sell products is through a distribution agreement. Usually (but certainly not always), the distributor you appoint will hold some stock and take responsibility for effectively reselling the product into a local market. Some distributors only obtain stock on a "call off" basis, i.e. only when they get an order in. On the one hand, this causes delays but on the other hand it keeps the distributors' costs low and means their exposure to holding stock is nil. The distributor will have no rights to make the product or use the trade mark / brand / packaging unless expressly in connection with selling your product. A marketing campaign and trade fairs may well be agreed between the parties. Indeed, it would be prudent to do so. In doing this both parties will know what their target markets are and have a common purpose of approach. Another consideration is for both parties to agree all branding use, point of sale items, brochures and website etc. It would normally be wrong for the distributor to repackage or rebrand the product unless that had been specifically agreed and other than for good reasons – i.e. to comply with local packaging and legal regulations. Be very wary of any distributor that wants to do this. It may be because they want to build their own brand and obtain a generic product at some later date – e.g. when your products come off patent.

Where distributors carry stock it is often wise to agree not only the stock levels they will carry but also the lead times for further supplies, or big orders. These types of issues depend on the products sold, but if the there are long lead times for manufacture and supply then both parties need to know where they stand. Bear in mind that products made in China for example, will have a lead time of at least six - eight weeks purely for the purposes of shipping them to the UK or Europe.

Distribution agreements can be short in duration (one or two years) and renewable only upon certain trigger sales levels being met. If the arrangement isn't working out it should be relatively easy to terminate the agreement, agree a short sell off period or repatriation of stock and for both parties to move on. There may be several distributors in any one market, and distribution agreements are a convenient way to penetrate new markets with relative ease using established partners on arms length terms. However, bear in mind there is little point in having a distributor unless there is already some demand locally for a product or service. Hence the need to work together in respect of marketing ideas.

What is a Reseller Agreement and why are they used?

These are a variation on distributor agreements and are quite common for the sales of software and certain technology. They are sometimes known as "Value Added Reseller" and even "Original Equipment Manufacturer" or "OEM agreements". For most resellers, the distributor is unlikely to hold much stock but they will often promote software / technology to a range of end users either in a particular market sector or as bundled package as part of a solution and service provided by the reseller. Where this arises the reseller may provide services such as support and technical back up which the software producer could not manage or can only manage on certain terms. The reseller scenario can add a great deal of value to the software /technology businesses, as a premium reseller often knows a great deal about the products they are selling and are experts in their field. As far as the software developer is concerned a good reseller can focus on a target area, sell new software into businesses and provide huge leverage to the developer. With the right software, or technology, these are win-win situations.

Original Equipment Manufacturer Agreements (OEMs)

OEM's often arise where mass produced components are integrated into other businesses goods. By way of example in the automotive industry certain components are used in the manufacture of a number of makes of car, for example, Skoda's are built with a range of VW parts. These types of arrangements frequently arise in electronics industries. The original manufacturer can make lower cost parts and these are effectively "branded" when put into other businesses equipment. The TV and telecoms industries use these types of agreements all the time. There is of course no point in reinventing the wheel!

What are Agency Agreements and why are they used?

These are frequently used in national and overseas trade. An agent is appointed to make sales in a particular territory and they rarely carry anything other than sample stock. The agent is, if you like, an outsourced sales person. Accordingly, if they are selling tangible products they're not usually in a position to fulfil any orders they take. Products and services are delivered from the principal for whom the agent acts. The agent can bind the principal into fulfilling orders from whoever they sell to; however, this isn't always what the principal would want, so agency agreements can have something of a downside in certain circumstances. The agent will take a percentage of sales and that "cut" may go on for several years after the sales process is established.

One problem with agents is ensuring they perform their sales function. A contract between agent and principal should ALWAYS be established and it should be possible for the principal to get rid of the non-performing agent relatively quickly and inexpensively. In the absence of a contract the termination consequences can be financially disastrous. Within the EU the situation is heavily regulated. Outside the EU agents may be able to register their agreements in the local courts, which means that if there is a dispute you can find yourself in court overseas with a justice system dependent on bribes to get the appropriate result.

The big advantage of having an agent on board is that the cost of appointing one is relatively low, and the right person is already likely to have good contacts in the region. They are also incentivised by making sales and obtaining results. If the commission is set at the right level it is a system that works well. Choose an agent who has not only good local contacts but also one that understands your technology and isn't selling a competitor product. Most agents act for a number of principals and they are the local "face" of your company. If they don't get it right and you have an agent who upsets your key customers, you can be excluded from key markets for some time after you've terminated their agreements. From what I've seen, one of the key mistakes principals make when appointing an agent is a lack of monitored supervision and support. Agents are only human; they need support and guidance, reminders and incentives just like the rest of us!

What are Collaboration Agreements and where are they used?

There are many instances where technology, goods or services would be improved by assistance from a third party. In fact, the technology may require a number of parties to work on it before it gets to market. These collaboration agreements are often found between academic institutions and companies. Many collaboration agreements have multiple parties. The most important factors to consider can be summarised as follows:

1. **Who is bringing what to the project?** What is the underlying IP and what exists or is being created? The asset being brought to a project is often defined as "background IP". In effect the agreement is bringing in a licence arrangement to use this background IP.

2. **Who gets to take stuff away?** Who will own the resulting IP and product rights and on what terms? The resulting IP may be a collaborative product or service using background IP from both parties but delivering it in a new way. It is very important that both parties agree at the outset how this is to be created and managed. Ownership and licensing or sharing that new product is critical to the success of it. Quite often one party is in a much better position to commercialise the resulting IP, or exploit it in a new market or arena. Accordingly, the terms of licensing and royalties back to other parties are very important for everyone. Where the collaboration is unsure of what will result from joint activities it is wise to build in review mechanisms. There is no point in getting to the end of the joint project and then having the debate!

3. **What is the scope of the project? Who will manage it and report on the progress?** Committees and regular feedback are vitally important features of such collaborative involvement. If you are working with a much larger partner, then their internal management systems will mandate feedback to the top people.

4. **What are the terms for payment /royalty or upfront lump sums? If parties to agreements ever fall out, then nine times out of ten it boils down to money.** It is the same with all contracts! However, again it can be good to build in a review mechanism that allows the parties to reflect on their positions and move forward collaboratively rather than fall out.

5. **Will there be milestones and timelines for when a party to the agreement can exit?** If the collaboration starts off with a joint project then it is vital that the scope of that project is agreed. It sounds easy but sometimes it is not. I've revisited a number of contracts for clients where we've been back and redefined things such as "foreground or resulting IP" before the project is finished. **Things change – be prepared for it.** Provided you all have the same longer term objectives, this doesn't really matter. It DOES matter if the commercial objectives of one party changes.

6. **If one party exits, then what are the terms of that early exit – for example exit before completion?** What seems like a great collaboration can change. Research objectives and funding allocations change. Businesses can find themselves tied into a project that they can no longer afford, nor does

it accord with their longer term commercial aspirations. However, if a project is incomplete who picks up the tab and what happens to the results? As with all things prevention is better than cure and often leads to a less acrimonious result.

The great advantage of collaborating can of course be the cost sharing aspect of getting something to market quickly and reliably when your business doesn't have all the right know-how.

Sometimes these arrangements become difficult as they require a crystal ball to predict all the possible outcomes. I've seen many university agreements that are quite opaque about the outcomes of a project! Issues arise if one party pulls out early. This often leaves the others to fill the technology gap and extra cost commitments.

There are dozens of versions of collaboration agreements. These types of agreements are often referred to as Joint Venture (JV) or partnerships. In legal terms JV's and partnerships are quite different so I'd urge you to be very cautious about the way you refer to working with another party. By way of example, a partnership agreement is governed in the UK by the Partnership Act and JV's usually indicate the formation of a jointly owned company of some kind. From a lawyer's perspective a JV may be something you'd consider if you were moving into an overseas market where the local restrictions meant you had to have a local corporate partner or indeed a local company through whom all local trade is channelled. This is increasingly rare but still occasionally arises. Collaborating with someone is not as onerous or complicated as a formal JV or Partnership Deed. It should leave original aspects of each collaborators business intact and it rarely requires detailed management from each party to make it work.

The type of collaborative contracts I most often encounter include marketing collaborations, revenue sharing arrangements, referral arrangements and a wide variety of internet based arrangements from white labelling to reselling. So, if you think working with another business can benefit both of you, but is best done at commercial arms length, then collaboration is for you.

What are Research and Development Agreements (R&Ds) and where are they used?

R&D agreements are frequently used by bigger organisations these days especially where they outsource part or whole research projects. Companies such as Rolls Royce increasingly use universities and similar institutions to undertake research. This has the advantage of cutting internal research costs for bigger companies and it returns the typical advantages seen in outsourcing, i.e. no need to permanently recruit expensive staff with specialist skills.

As for collaboration agreements, there may well be several parties all with different expertise, and certainly different background IP. Many of the comments for collaboration agreements therefore also apply here. A few variations of this type of agreement include "inventors agreements" where individual inventors work on a project or share a royalty stream and "key supplier" agreements, where certain suppliers provide key materials for a project. There are many variations on all the agreements mentioned above. Warranties and indemnities may be required by some parties, and royalty rates will vary hugely – this is a book topic in its own right as royalties vary so much from one industry to the next, so it's important to get expert legal advice to ensure your protection.

Why sell goods and services directly?

Thanks to the Internet it has never been easier to trade nationally and internationally. Getting your terms and conditions right is however a challenge that many businesses overlook until they have a dispute. Disputes often arise over two things, namely the payment and delivery of the goods. Payment can be complicated by cheques bouncing, credit cards being dishonestly used, or payment being taken more than once. The delivery of goods is often covered by the distance selling regulations, and particular care has to be taken over some consumer items. These include clothing, food and items such as beds or bedding.

Be aware, consumer regulations change regularly and it is worthwhile making sure that your standard terms are updated every year or so and that the consumer has actually had the opportunity to see and accept or decline them. They should also be written in plain English. If the customer can't find your terms, or doesn't understand them, how can they be deemed to have accepted them? Plus, you need to consider what happens if your customers are unhappy with the goods sold? Who is responsible for the delivery of goods? Are they insured in transit? What sign off terms do you have for accepting that things are delivered to the right address and in good order?

One of the main draw backs to selling online is payment fraud. I've had many clients who've ended up with large claw backs from credit card companies and others who've lost a great deal of stock to unscrupulous consumers who've dishonestly paid for goods with someone else's credit card. Be aware of this when you set up a website and make sure, not only that your terms and conditions cover key points, but also that you have procedures in place to counter the dishonest customer. In fact, increasingly, a number of payment services or merchant services offered by banks and similar financial institutions insist on you having professionally drafted terms and conditions of sale on websites and for telephone transactions.

Why bother getting a lawyer to do your agreements?

I've heard many people ask why they should get a lawyer to do their agreements. Whilst I acknowledge that for many small companies legal fees may be a burden, a good lawyer will help you make the most of any deal and will help you avoid the elephant traps which will lose you money. Even some business people and entrepreneurs, who openly dislike lawyers, usually have a trusted legal advisor in the background somewhere to help make decisions. They may not tell you this but Donald Trump and Alan Sugar always have their legal advisors on speed dial! Some of my most loyal clients came to me after they failed to take legal advice or use suitable agreements. However, if you're a small business, then as a rule of thumb, if any contract is going to be worth more than £50,000 to your company then use a lawyer – always. I can't afford to lose £50,000 and I don't know anyone or any business that would willingly expose themselves to that kind of loss. The losses aren't always that straight forward or obvious either. For example, management time and loss of reputation / goodwill often go hand in hand with contracts going sour. Another important issue is dealing with the general public. Consumer contracts need to be thought over and the landscape of consumer contracts changes regularly. Understandably, specific protection is given to the public, especially in relation to the Sale of Goods Act and Consumer

Credit regulations etc. So, if you're trading with the public you need to be aware of the strength of consumers' rights.

What can go wrong when you don't get a solicitor involved

A salutary lesson from recent UK banking history… Another hidden trap for businesses is that well drafted contracts considerably enhance the value of any company. When a business is offered for sale, a potential buyer will look not just at the finances, but they will often spend a considerable amount of money on a due diligence report from their lawyers. A well thought through report will highlight the legal strengths and weaknesses of the target company. It will flush out things such as short term contracts or ones that will terminate soon and not be renewed. These types of contracts may well reduce the company's value. In fact, since the 'credit crunch' and deep economic recession of 2008, due diligence should be of major importance. It should be remembered that it was the Royal Bank of Scotland's lamentable and poor to non-existent due diligence during the acquisition of the Dutch Bank ABN Amro that led to the collapse of the whole bank. Even the big players get it badly wrong sometimes.

Well drafted contracts considerably enhance such things as revenue streams – especially in technology companies.

If you buy a company without doing proper due diligence, then get used to encountering surprises. Most of them unpleasant. I recall the sale of one internet company back in early 2000 that appeared on paper to have many more fee paying customers than it actually had. The frankly appalling billing and financial systems it had nearly took the company down post sale. The sellers had gone off with their millions and of course had not agreed to any warranties or indemnities.

The buyers had not asked their lawyers to do a full due diligence report and the skeletons were falling over themselves to exit the closet once key members of staff left the company in the weeks following the acquisition. The unscrupulous sellers, who had, presumably, seen the writing on the wall, had deliberately rushed the deal through and had brow beaten the buyers in a rising market where everyone wanted a slice of the Internet action so to speak. In their haste to obtain what appeared to be a plum business, the buyers had taken what they believed to be a calculated risk. In fact they had bought a company that was in dire trouble – it took over 18 months and a whole new financial team to bring it back into line, deal with the outstanding customer complaints and outstanding VAT issues. The resulting loss of confidence in the company and angry double billed customers meant that the company had to rebrand before it could rebuild confidence and its shaky customer base. It happens – don't let it happen to you!

Step 8
Balancing the Books

Money does strange things to people. It is true. I've always known it but as a solicitor, I get to see what happens all too clearly all too often. Money means different things to different people and it triggers some very basic emotions and insecurities. Money can make people greedy, lazy or both. It can make people fearful. It can incentivise and galvanise but it can also demotivate and destroy. I've learnt much more about this subject since running my own business too. Mostly the hard way! Things I wish I'd known about money when I started my business were as follows:

1. **The importance of budgeting and forecasting.** It is vital to know exactly where you are and where you want to be.

2. **The importance of paying for good advice from an expert** rather than searching the Internet or relying on press or Government departments and taking heed of accepted "truths" from friends, well-wishers and ill-informed staff. These sources often turn out to be at worst completely wrong or at best only partially correct.

3. **Know what is coming into and going out of your business accounts.** If you don't overheads can creep up – as can tax bills. They will leave you high and dry!

4. **Have a contingency fund** to deal with the unexpected. Let's call it the "Shit Happens" fund – because it does!

5. **Keep on top of your accounts** – don't let bookkeeping entries slip behind. This is especially important if you are VAT registered in the UK. The tax man may wait for your income tax but the VAT and National Insurance must be paid. If you are late you will receive punitive surcharges. Her Majesties Revenue and Customs (HMRC) views your payable tax as "their money" – especially VAT, and it is due when it is due – not when you've got the cash flow to forward it to them to pay it. Oh, and the VAT man can close you down overnight – even if you are a limited company! The only exceptions to this appear to be very big corporations, who get away with part payments of tax. Seems unfair doesn't it? - DON'T get me on my soap box on this one… In the majority of cases, unless you're running a very big company, this rarely applies to YOU.

6. **Don't bank roll other businesses** by giving them extended credit; making payments on their behalf or failing to chase them up when they owe you money. This simply exposes your business to unsustainable risk. My business is regulated by the Solicitors Regulatory Authority or SRA and we have strict policies about this. We still get it wrong from time to time.

7. **Know the value in your business** – people, IP and assets. Ask yourself where your income is coming from and why? With IP ask yourself what is unique about what you do. What is important in distinguishing your business from others? If business has declined or you're not getting paid, ask yourself some tough questions and face the unpalatable answers. Service levels may have slipped, goods are not that desirable, staff aren't performing, your IP is being copied or is outdated etc.

8. **Know the difference between commodities and service.** Buy commodities on comparative cost – paper supplies are pretty much the same from any supplier. Service is a totally different matter. You can buy a cheap flight if you wish and with all the added extras but lose a few hours at the airport and you may well have paid out as much as a more expensive flight – not to mention the cost to your temper as you're treated like cattle. This is because the cheap airlines have cut all the flesh off their service and don't care about your trip. They care about the extras you buy to make up their margins. It is more so with some advisors who may or may not know what they're doing. More of which later.

9. **Keep an eye on overheads.** Always. By that I don't mean be tight fisted about everything but you'd be amazed at how wasteful people can be when it isn't their money that is being spent.

'A cynic is a man who knows the price of everything, and the value of nothing.'

Oscar Wilde

It may be me but I just can't stand bad service. If you are going to serve me food or a drink then serve me promptly, politely, provide me with something decent and take my hard earned cash with a smile. It is my money and I've chosen to spend it – not give it away.

Sadly a number of businesses and professionals have forgotten this fundamental, possibly old fashioned courtesy. They will take your money, not communicate with you fully and then do the job badly. In times of recession in particular many jobs have been de-skilled to the lowest level to cut costs. It is not unusual to find out that your work is done by barely qualified staff with inadequate supervision. Sadly some practices put junior people on tasks that even senior staff aren't familiar with. Getting rid of them when they've made a mistake can be easier than getting rid of someone more senior who shouldn't have agreed to do it in the first place. Don't get caught out by this. I'm a great believer in staff development– but they do need to be properly trained and supervised or they will end up costing you money. Find out who will be doing your legal work and how much experience and supervision they have. Ask the question whether the practice or the individual has the skills to do it in the first place. Just because a professional tells you they can do it, it doesn't mean that they actually can.

Make sure you get a "like for like" quote on work. Some law firms' patent and trade mark attorneys have radically different charging structures. What appears to be a "better deal" often isn't, as every extra letter, email and phone call will be added to your bill. Fee earners in these practices often have fee targets and an extra few pounds on each file will contribute towards that target. Ask for an estimate of fees up front and find out exactly what is or is not included. Of course none of us are mind readers and things do crop up that weren't budgeted for but much of the cost should broadly follow the budget laid down, If it doesn't the professional should advise you why things aren't going to plan. We at Virtuoso Legal always provide quotes before doing any work and we even provide detailed budgets for any litigation we undertake. This can mean we give our clients ball park figures for each stage but at least then the ups and downs can be accounted for and predicted. Don't misunderstand me – the unexpected can and does crop up. It is rarely possible to be 100 % accurate, but at least where possible you should be informed at every stage why costs increase or change.

In today's internet age not everything is as it seems. Let me give you an example…

Client A came to me with a business project which looked excellent. All he had to do was to secure exclusive rights to the manufacturing process and get the brand right. Money was tight. Goods were being imported by the container load from the Far East to keep manufacturing costs low and to keep cost per item at rock bottom. By the time goods had been bought and were being shipped, there wasn't much to spend on branding and marketing. A brand name was chosen and came back clear with a clearance search. We filed a trade mark. After two months our chosen mark was opposed by a big US corporation – the reason was an issue that did not emerge on a clearance search. Rather than spend money on defending it (we advised the client that they had a good case but the client had been told by a friend that it wasn't a great mark anyway…) my client decided to abandon the brand name. My client then went online to find the cheapest possible trade mark filing. He felt he had spent enough on lawyers and just wanted to get his trade mark registered. He was not advised to do a clearance search by his online supplier – in fact he was told that he didn't need one! If the online organisation didn't get the mark he wanted, they told him wouldn't have to pay a filing fee. Understandably, he thought this was a good offer.

Two months later, client A got a "cease and desist" letter telling him not to sell his newly branded goods, as they were classed as "passing off" and infringing someone else's trade mark. Client A was indeed and very sadly squarely in the wrong. Even a simple Google search would have shown him a conflicting prior mark. However, by that time he had £100,000 in stock in a warehouse waiting to be sold. All packed and branded with the new branding but no way could he sell any of it! When client A looked to the online trade mark registration company, he found out that not only had they a disclaimer in their terms for his losses, but also that they had no professional indemnity insurance. They were quite clearly not on the hook for his significant losses, which included most of his product, which was unsellable, but also all of his marketing spend for the product launch.

The Internet and deregulation has opened up the market hugely. The idea was to give consumers choice. In fact in some respects, all that has happened is that a plethora of online services have been set up which purport to do legal services – such as filing your trade marks when they have no expertise in doing so, providing ill fitting contracts or registering copyright material, which isn't required to protect it! Many of these businesses are unregulated and appear at the top of searches, as without the burden of regulation and the costs associated with it, they can and do spend lots of money on website optimising and Google AdWords to propel their website listings to the top. More disturbing is the poor quality advice people are offered. Many have no professional indemnity insurance.

"Price is what you pay,

value is what you get."
Warren Buffet

FACT:

If you want good, reliable, expert service, then you have to pay a decent fee for it.

Money saving tips when you work with professional advisors and solicitors:

1. If you have a dispute, always gather a complete audit trail of events. Take the whole history, emails, copies of contracts, copies of early design drawings etc. with you when see your solicitor at a first meeting. Even better forward a pack of information to them before you meet.

2. Before you do meet, clarify any charges associated with the meeting / review. Many professionals – including my legal practice, do a free or discounted first meeting to flush out the issues.

3. Ask for a written estimate of the stages of any job. Make sure you know what is in each stage.

4. Ask for a checklist to keep YOU on track and focused. We

invariably use checklists with clients, especially when it comes to negotiating contracts. The headings keep everyone's eyes on the key clauses.

5. Ask your solicitor for advice BEFORE you start negotiations. A specialist solicitor will often be a good source of commercial advice on issues such as royalty rates, duration of the agreement and what other key commercial terms should be negotiated alongside the checklist headings. This is where a good solicitor can add enormous value to your business.

6. If your usual solicitor doesn't regularly deal with this area of law then don't be afraid to ask for either another solicitor in the same firm or seek out a specialist in a different practice. My accountant always refers me to a tax specialist if that is the advice he knows I need. The same should apply to the law.

7. Honesty and integrity are two "non-negotiable" traits in dealing with any professional. If you feel uneasy about the advice you've been given then question it. **It is your money and your business,** however, don't opinion shop around with dozens of advisors. If you've been told something you don't like, as it doesn't accord with your wishes, it doesn't mean the professional is wrong. Feel confident about those you instruct but if the relationship does break down (sometimes they do) move on, and move on quickly. In my experience complaining after the event is far too late. For some reason people are reluctant to change advisors. Usually the fear is associated with cost – people are scared that someone else will charge more for picking up the file, but nothing is more

expensive than bad advice! I know as I've paid for it in the past. My gut instinct told me to move on for a reason but I stuck it out and in return I almost lost everything I'd worked for.

8. Finally in this day and age the whole legal arena has been opened up to competition. Whilst this has, in some cases driven down cost, it has also driven down value and capability. There are numerous ways in which people will take money from you and provide a poor or even a bad service. We've all been seduced by it. Sometimes it works and sometimes not but find out first what qualifications and what experience your advisors have and what credibility they have with clients and others. Shop around, ask for references and talk to people. Look on things such as the Law Society Website or similar professional directories.

Stages to look for in any quotes for fees

Trade Marks

- UK Clearance and filing in 2 or 3 classes.

- Community Trade Marks Clearance and filing in up to 3 classes

- International Trade Marks **USA, India and Canada**

- Worldwide – using a Madrid protocol filing it is possible to save some money and obtain coverage in key markets such as the USA, Japan, China and Australia.

Patents

- UK Clearance searches UK filing

- European

- Worldwide - this can vary hugely according to where you need cover.

- Agreement costs

- Licensing budget

- Franchising / complex licensing

- Assignments and non-disclosure agreements and International assignments.

Litigation

Intellectual Property and Enterprise Court (IPEC) – deals with all kinds of IP disputes, but especially infringement actions. It has specialist Judges and bespoke procedures including small claims procedure. This was previously known as the Patents County Court or PCC. It uses capped fees and capped damages costs.

High Court IP litigation

Budget legal costs depending on complexity and type of case. Your legal case will cost more if you have lots of defendants, complex facts, extensive disclosure evidence and expert witnesses.

There is no cap on damages in the High court but the vast majority of claims involve damages **of less** than £1 million.

Costs and company protection

There can be good legal reasons why IP is held by either a holding Company or individuals. You'd be well advised to put in place a licence between the holding company and the company that uses the IP. In the absence of such a licence, IP rights can be difficult to enforce and it may be that damages are difficult to recover. The holding company usually pays the filing and protection costs in return for royalties. The holding company may well benefit from tax breaks in a number of ways, such as the Patent Box scheme.

Insurance for IP litigation

A variety of insurers now offer both before the event and after the event legal expenses insurance for IP related claims. As a regulated law firm Virtuoso Legal are nominated by some insurers to do IP litigation. We are also authorised by the Solicitors Regulatory Authority or SRA in respect of helping people find insurance for the legal costs. This means that SME's can afford to protect their IP where as otherwise they'd find the legal expenses too much for them to bear. I'd strongly advise looking at this type of help.

Small Companies and individual inventors

There is a great deal of advice out there for smaller companies. You will find that organisations such as the Patent Office – www.ipo.gov.uk provide quite a lot of free information and searching. However, be aware that their staff are not legally qualified and whilst I've often found they bend over backwards to help individuals, they are NOT practitioners and can often miss vital issues. UK entrepreneur

Trevor Baylis also runs a website and supports small inventors and companies. Trevor truly flies the flag for inventors in the UK – see www.trevorbaylisbrands.com. However, the Internet has sprung up some less well meaning or indeed less well informed types of websites. It is such a shame. The British are often an eclectic mix of the world's best inventors but the world's worst protectors and exploiters of IP. Time and time again we come up with brilliant ideas and concepts which wither on the vine as there is no funding and indeed insufficient drive to make them happen. Some big corporations do have the facilities to review and examine ideas and proposals, yet many do not. Some which do include Black and Decker – who of course bought the highly successful WorkMate® from an individual inventor many years ago. You will also need to be cautious who you show things to. Make sure they sign a non-disclosure agreement before you show them everything they need to see to evaluate an idea.

Bear in mind too that most of the larger companies are NOT interested in mere ideas. They will want to see hard evidence of the products you are proposing. This may well mean building at least a well made working prototype or having some good experimental results. Big companies are more interested in collaboration and risk sharing than developing things alone. This has advantages for both parties as it means you can both be part of bringing something to market; however, if you are the smaller party be aware that commercially you may have little say in how things are done.

Summary

"Value rather than price has made me rich… what you don't know keeps you poor."
Robert Kiyosaki - *Rich Dad, Poor Dad*

Don't get too emotional about money – see it as your servant, not your master. Think about the value of things – not the cost of obtaining good advice. **Making money will follow from taking well thought through business decisions.**

Step 9
The Internet and IP Procurement

Or how businesses must "do"
business to survive

Every now and then a "game-changer" business is created. Tim Berners Lee did that with the Internet. I was in practice before the Internet became the world resource it is today. I remember the early days of email when few people had a website and many law firms didn't have a computer for each fee earner. Laughable now of course. Fax machines were commonly used and our post bags were full of 'snail mail', which, as dutiful solicitors, we responded to on paper. It is a world away from where we are now, although I do believe that many businesses still haven't really embraced the information technology (IT) revolution and moved with the times.

There are still some solicitors who don't use scan and email for correspondence and UK courts will still only receive small size documents by email. There are online court services such as online issues for small claims — but contested claims are always a problem for automated systems. In fact, only the other day a businessman said to me, please don't email me as I'm not that comfortable with it. I did wonder where he had been for the last 15 years! That situation, of course, is very rare and I do encourage my team to TALK to people above and before electronic communication. Talking builds relationships, email rarely does that.

I also remember the birth of eBay and thinking who would want to buy second hand stuff without actually seeing it first. I couldn't believe that women would buy clothing that they'd never seen or tried on. I'll admit it; I NEVER saw the all encompassing power of this technology at its birth. I was like most people, way behind the curve when it came to foreseeing the future and how IT would reshape many businesses. I'm still not an "early adopter" of technology, simply because the first version of anything rarely works that well. Sadly, it seems, many software companies launch into selling before making a product or website fool proof.

Today, it is simply unthinkable to have a world without internet technology. We in the West gawp at people who don't have IT systems and wonder how they cope, yet it's a fact that at the time of going to press around two thirds of the world's population are still not regularly connected to the Internet. These people tend to be part of the poorer emerging nations with large populations and because they're not on our doorstep we don't consider them. But, we ignore it at our peril. As we've seen in the Middle East, people using smart phones accessing social media sites, including Twitter and Facebook, have helped orchestrate the impetus to topple political regimes and exposed tragedy and hypocrisy in a way that conventional newspapers and TV channels could only dream of. What will these people do when they use the Internet for business? That will be a game changer for them too where business is still done on a face to face, know each other basis, I believe they will find the changes extraordinarily difficult to cope with.

Whilst it is unthinkable for us now to do business without the Internet, this technology has spawned a whole range of scams and opportunities in equal measure. If there is one area of my practice that challenges us daily, then it is the Internet. Take the call I had the other day from a hotel group. Their websites had been ripped off by a rogue website. Copyright material including photographs and text had been slavishly copied. In this case the issue wasn't because the rogue website had overtaken the authentic website at the top of Google's search engine, it was because the rogue duplicate site sent online searchers through an affiliate programme which paid the rogue website owner a referral fee for bookings through a look-alike website that the online customer would probably be completely unaware of.

Spoof sites abound, selling everything from counterfeit drugs to illicit banking sites with phishing scams to capture your financial details or clone you online to rip you off. If you want to take medication that you've bought from the Internet, then you must take the associated risks. These include getting the wrong dose of an active ingredient to taking tablet, "fillers" that can cause an allergic reaction – or worse. Even in my own profession, all is not as it seems. It is easy to trap the public. A solicitor is a solicitor as far as most of the public are concerned, and one looks pretty much the same as another. However, any number of unregulated lookalike businesses abound. But if it isn't regulated by the Solicitors Regulatory Association or SRA, then they're not accredited and governed by the Law Society regulator.

Common traps when trading online

Let's first of all look at some of the common traps people fall into when taking their business online. Dealing with website or software developers is the first hurdle to cross. Over the years I have had numerous complaints from clients that what their website developer has promised, hasn't been delivered. It all comes down to one thing – planning and having a contract in place. I'll give you an example – and this lady has become a real friend after her experience with one developer. Let's call her "Jane". Jane had worked in the City of London's financial sector for years. She'd made money and saw herself as an entrepreneur. After leaving work with a large pay off Jane decided that she'd start her own luxury goods website; taking all the lovely things you can buy in interior design and furniture shops and put them online. Now Jane was no fool. She'd worked in business for years and seen them succeed and fail. She carefully planned the goods she'd sell and spent months finding the right products and the right suppliers to deal with. She had good PR contacts too. She touted around for a website company who could design a suitable website with online payment provisions and a reporting facility that would tell her when to order more stock.

After choosing her web developer, the developer obtained a domain name for Jane's website (in our case our domain name or URL is www.virtuosolegal.com) and put together a visually attractive website, which appeared to work. Jane launched her website with great acclaim and, thanks to her fabulous PR campaign she had extensive nationwide coverage for her new business. But the problem quickly emerged that her website couldn't process many orders! Yes, that's right, you got your credit card out to buy your lovely new and expensive things and the website blew you off the payment page. Repeatedly.

What's more, the stock that was sold was never replaced, as the system couldn't report back what had been ordered! Sadly, that was only part of the problem with the website developer. Jane had invested all her money in marketing and PR in the honest belief that once set up the website would simply function as she had outlined to the developer. It didn't. Due to the fact that Jane had no contract with the web developer she also got charged for every last change she had to make to get the website to operate correctly and couldn't get her domain name back to move her website to another developer until, in my opinion, she'd paid a 'ransom' fee. Whilst eventually Jane did move her business to another website developer lasting damage had been done to her reputation.

Sadly I've heard this story so many times in various guises we therefore provide a checklist for clients who want to move their business online, or who want to improve their online services.

The key pointers for a website contract are these:

1. Your contract should cover the functionality of the website – make sure if you want online payment that the details of this or other important things such as warehousing, or keeping customer details are contractually covered.

2. **Agree what changes will or will not be charged for**. Many developers these days will either let you change your own material or agree to do so much for fixed fees. Agree any provisions for changes.

3. With a website you are not paying for the overheads of a shop or some expensive premises BUT **good systems and experienced web developers are rarely cheap** options to start with. Online and offline retailer businesses do sit well together if they work in tandem – look at John Lewis, Next, Argos and others. It is about getting the combination of

shopping experience right for all your potential customers.

4. **Own your own domain name and ensure you know the password and log in details for it.** The same also applies for any social media log ins! It sounds blindingly obvious but I wish I had a fiver for every aggrieved business owner I've spoken to who DIDN'T do this. One of my client's instructed a one man band developer who disappeared off the face of the earth, owning and taking with him, not only her domain name, but also all the log in details.

5. **Agree where your website should be hosted.** The hosting you agree to may have to change depending on the business you do and the volume of traffic it generates.

6. **Spell out and agree back end functionality in detail.** If you want a complex customer relationship management (CRM) or online payment system setting up, make sure your developer knows what they're doing, and contractually bind them into delivering it. There are many very good software platforms out there these days. Few websites need building from scratch, unless they are completely bespoke designs with very specific functionality requirements.

7. **Agree a timetable for delivery and if required have sign off and delivery provisions.** Complicated back end systems may take weeks or months to get right. Don't sign off delivery of these until they work as you've agreed in your specification. N.B. If you're site is going to be complicated allow for realistic development time and testing in consultation with your developer.

8. **Agree a "walk away" provision – even before you've started.** I know it sounds cynical. It is a bit like a pre-nuptial agreement, but like marriage, not every business relationship ends in success and both parties can get bitter and twisted. If your web or software developer can't deliver, then make sure you can take what's been done and paid for to a third party.

There are of course many other things to consider when setting up your website. In particular your domain name or URL, which can become a valuable IP asset in its own right. Whilst something descriptive works well for searching and optimisation of a particular product or service, bear in mind that it will be easy to imitate and plagiarise. By way of example "holiday bookings" is similar to "holiday lettings" as a domain name and neither of them are likely to be available to you as a trade mark as they're too descriptive.

My experience with website owners is that Google pay per click and optimising your website for visibility is often very worthwhile. For some reason many business owners still haven't woken up to this.

In my mind doing both are essential, although, and Google won't like me saying this, Google seems to prefer its own customers when it comes to organic searches. I realise I may get some grief for saying this but this is my third party experience. If that is the case, then Google would be no different from many printed publishing houses that have always put the interests of paying advertisers first. So let's face facts, there is no moral high ground here, despite what anyone tells you.

Once your website is planned and commissioned, you then have to think about how to do business. It is vitally important that you get some things in good order. Your website terms of business will always be the start point. How is payment taken online? When is the contract formed and concluded – after email confirmation or at delivery? This is a vital point to get right, as when your website posts the wrong prices by accident, you'll be scurrying to read the small print! What about the Distance Selling Regulations? When and under what circumstances will goods be returned and refunded? What do your terms say about insurance or delivery costs? How do you know the person who ordered the goods is actually the one paying for them? I've dealt with all these types of problems and more! It is really important to get it right. Fraud on the Internet is rife and charge backs for credit card payments can be a crippling blow to cash flow.

Other things which spring to mind are privacy policies, and data protection. If you keep information on payment or credit checks etc., you will need the appropriate data protection registration. The Information Commissioners website has a great deal of useful information on it – use it – it's free! www.ico.gov.uk   By way of example it has great guidance on the use of CCTV in public places. Also, remember that a wide variety of people may use your website. Make it easy to use and accessible and therefore useable by people with certain disabilities – see the Disability Discrimination Act.

Legislation is in place that says your website must comply with such things as the Distance Selling Regulations and many others. UK businesses also benefit from doing a great deal of international trade online, with the UK being the distribution hub and logistics centre for many well-known online fashion brands. Next and others are past masters at getting an easy to use website deliver desirable products quickly. Have a look at their websites and marketing campaigns and you'll see why.

Social Media

No good marketing campaign would be complete these days without the use of social media to sell any goods and services. Websites such as Trip Advisor, Facebook and Twitter to name but a few can make or break businesses. If you don't know about them I encourage you to read up on how you can use them to your benefit, both for talking to your customers and for listening to them - ignore them at your peril. As a business owner, I've found it informative, fun and useful to get young trainees and interns to look at this in detail.

Your business IT strategy and why it is so important

I really can't think of many businesses these days that aren't reliant on their IT. Retailing, logistics, banking, manufacturing, aviation – you name it, businesses of all sectors, sizes and description would sink without the right IT systems to make them work. Years ago I recall taking a phone call from a major Plc client who was being held to ransom by their IT supplier. The in-house solicitor was at his wits end. The new IT system, which governed all the warehousing, delivery, customer records and payments, was all under the control of one software system and one IT supplier who hadn't quite got some parts of the commission right. It had 'bugs'– which meant that my client, who had implemented the new IT system, had delivery and performance issues.

In order to rectify this, my client stopped paying the instalments due under the contract for the delivery of the software. In return the IT supplier threatened to turn off the whole system. Had they done so (and contractually they had the right to do so), they would have thrown my client's business into chaos. My advice was clear – pay up and then argue because you've no right under your contract to do anything else. Then renegotiate your contract! A contract containing simple sign off procedures and some decent beta testing before final payments would have dealt with most of these issues and the dispute wouldn't have arisen as catastrophically as it did.

Years later the same thing happened to a hotel group I was acting for. During the recent recession, they'd had cash flow problems and had stopped paying some suppliers, including their IT service suppliers. There's a lesson here!

Your IT supplier can stitch you up even faster than the Inland Revenue – and that's saying something!

So, what do you need to know to try and avoid these problems? Well let's start with the fundamentals – the specification of the system. If you need your new IT system to carry out specific tasks, then say so upfront. Adding on extras as you go along is madness. It is akin to asking a builder to build you a house and then telling him three months into the project that you need four bedrooms and not two. In fact IT systems have a lot in common with construction contracts.

If you are having a house built to a high specification, you will need to consider each detail up front. What will the windows look like, how many electric sockets will you need?

There is a real art in itemising software systems so that they work in accordance with your demands. Also, if you ask for too much functionality in one system, you stand a real risk of it not working as you require. If in doubt keep it simple. Specify the functionality according to your needs and make sure you can build in a little 'future proofing' to help ensure the system can be added to in due course. It is sometimes easier to bolt on and add functionality than it is to get it all right first time. It is easier if your IT supplier is aware of any future plans – they may be able to do many clever things but mind reading won't be one of them. IT contractors sometimes also like to promote the software packages that THEY supply. These aren't necessarily the ones that YOU need. Check and shop around.

Once you've decided what your systems need to do, look at the planning and implementation process. Engineers have always used Gant charts for large projects. IT projects should be the same. Do it in bite size chunks and keep it simple. I see over complex IT systems all the time. The end result is that end users are slow adopters of the technology and improvements and investments in IT are slow to show a real return on investment.

Once the overall architecture of the system is decided on and a project time line in place, make sure your contract, as a minimum, covers payments in instalments, delivery and acceptance sign off, and functionality change provisions. Ensure maintenance and improvements can be undertaken at reasonable costs and ensure you'll always have access to the programmers who really matter and not just the sales man or account executive who sold you the stystem in the first place.

I've met a number of IT directors in my time who hadn't

documented much, if any of what was going on – especially with a big procurement contract or as a business grew and needed complex IT implementing over time. When they left, (often sacked for being useless) no one could find out what software licences the company had, nor any contracts regarding commissioning or implementation and performance of the systems already in use. You see IT directors are human and like all humans some of them lack the capacity to organise themselves, but I know lots of astonishingly clever people who are lousy at organising things – especially themselves.

To make these things easy for businesses we put together checklists for negotiating and implementing IT contracts. Why have a contract? Well why would you spend hundreds of thousands of pounds on software but not set out the terms on which you are acquiring it – especially when your business depends on it. Of course using lawyers and making sure contracts are signed isn't a fool proof way of making sure your IT system will work as you so desire, but they're worth their weight in gold when it goes wrong and you can establish an audit chain of responsibility in order to fix things.

Owning the software

Another question I'm regularly asked by business owners is "do I own the software" to which the usual answer is "no". That confuses the hell out of business people who've often paid a great deal for bespoke systems and yet only ever get a licence to use them. In addition, they don't own the source code and can't usually change suppliers quickly when things go wrong. Be aware that Programmers rarely hand away rights to the code away as they re-use code and concepts all the time. Having software that you own outright invariably weights the price, as does having access to the source code and doing your own amendments and changes. If you need to do that, then negotiate it upfront. If your software supplier goes to the wall and you need access to the source code for your software, then make sure you've entered into an escrow agreement with them whereby a trigger event such as insolvency of an IT supplier means that your support is NOT compromised.

Organisations such as the NCC Group in Manchester can be a useful backup as independent holders of business critical source code.

Clearly, they charge for the service that they offer but many customers are happy to pay their fees in order to secure the rights to source code and ensure continuity of service. The NCC also has other services, such as securely holding data, and website performance testing. See www.nccgroup.com

Step 10
Counterfeiting and Copying
The costs and the extent of the problem…

Perhaps after writing this book someone will finally explain to me why some brand owners simply don't take any interest in the lucrative business of counterfeiting. I suspect that many don't think of it is a major problem, or that it doesn't really have a significant cost impact in their business. Why? If someone was ripping money off my bottom line or piggy-backing off all the hard work I've put into my business, then I'd be first in line to put a stop to it as quickly as possible. The issue appears to be that brand owners find this trade difficult to quantify and expensive to police.

The real business problem is that the damage is insidious, intangible and long term.

It is estimated that around 5% of all sales of products worldwide are counterfeit and that is one hell of a lot of trade! The further bad news is that around 90% of those counterfeit goods originate from

Chinese factories. The Chinese won't thank me for saying it, but I'm afraid it is true. It isn't as if the Chinese don't recognise and address it – they deal with it in a draconian way, handing down prison sentences for offenders, and summarily closing down factories that churn these goods out. The real truth is that the offenders are often difficult to track down and in any event the Chinese being the entrepreneurs that they are see one factory closing down as another person's opportunity: close one place down and another simply opens up just down the road from the closed factory. Please adjust your cultural glasses and see things as they do. They see it as a straightforward business opportunity; a business need waiting to be filled and paid for by Westerners who want fake goods and don't care about the source.

This has become such an issue that many luxury goods are no longer made in China. It has also become a big problem and barrier to international trade, with Microsoft and others carefully monitoring activities in China and political dialogue at a high level. The Chinese can and do make quality products but the costs of keeping an audit trail of product is just too difficult, complex and expensive for some Western companies to keep up. The tricks and scams are endless but the biggest one is production over run. In a vastly over simplified way this works as follows:

Factory 1 orders 1000 metres of cloth to make 500 dresses.

The factory owner knows that with careful pattern cutting they can make 600 dresses.

The brand owner allows 5% as "spoiled goods", i.e. dresses that will be rejected because of finish quality, so the brand owner only expects to ship 475 dresses.

Brand owner inspects and ships 475 dresses and factory owner sells 125 dresses out of the back door of the factory.

Easy isn't it? The same factory, the same fabric, the same manufacturing processes, often the same label – all at virtually no cost to the factory owner. And all very difficult to back. He or she is much hungrier and possibly poorer than you. Why WOULDN'T he do it? In many respects China is still an under developed nation – average wages are pitifully low and the incentive to cheat and improve your lot in life is high. The Chinese are nothing if not ambitious and that applies elsewhere in developing the world. You can add into that mix the fact that the justice system is less than reliable sometimes, so many individuals make enough money to keep them OUT of prison by bribery and corruption. This scam is often virtually undetectable unless rigorously audited systems and local management is in place to combat fraud. For one luxury brand owner that came to me, the only way they found out was when a supplier of their goods emerged in Africa. They didn't have a supplier there but you could certainly buy their dresses thanks to a flourishing trade in back door supply of over runs.

Many of the bigger accountancy firms will help police and audit these kinds of scams, and they're certainly good at their jobs. Employing a local person as your representative, or even better sending one of your staff over to inspect and review what is going on, will often pay dividends. However, don't be naive **not only is this eroding your profit margins, it is devaluing your brand.** Because of a market flooded with cheap imitations the luxury brand Burberry's exclusivity suffered heavily until they implemented a tough stance on counterfeit Burberry check designs. They fought hard to win back their name of elite tailoring but I hesitate to even take a guess at what it must have cost them. Here is a story from my colleague John Eastwood of Eiger Law – a specialist law firm in the Far East providing assistance to companies trading out there. John helped a UK software company minimise the risks of trading in China:

"In working with companies on the protection of their intellectual property in the Greater China region (the People's Republic of China, Hong Kong, Macau and Taiwan), it can be essential to look at corporate and commercial structures closely, particularly with regards to any goods or services being marketed into the People's Republic of China (PRC). It's quite common for foreign rights holders to work with local partners to use their knowledge of local market conditions and sales channels, but it is also important not to lose control of one's brand. In the heat of a possible business deal, foreign rights holders have been known to take the one-stop-shop perspective on local business partners to extremes, allowing them to register domain names and even trademarks in the local business partner's own name. In joint-venture activities with a local partner, it is also important for a foreign rights holder to retain some control over the local entity so as to protect their rights.

"For example, in working with a UK-headquartered software company planning to partner up with a major PRC company, we steered them away from the original plan to set up a PRC-based joint venture to handle all the sales and post-sales maintenance activities. Instead, to help the client exert more control, we came up with a different structure featuring a joint-venture corporate entity in Hong Kong, where the investor protections are much stronger and corporate operations are substantially more transparent. The Hong Kong joint-venture entity would then own a wholly-owned foreign entity (WOFE) in the PRC to handle the software sales and distribution. Because putting the software maintenance into the control of the local PRC partner would have allowed them to potentially get rid of the foreign rights holder and proceed on their own, we then provided for the client to instead set up a separate WOFE entity of its own to handle all post-sales maintenance services. The result was a structure that avoided centralization of power and control into the hands of a local distribution partner."

Where ever you are considering setting up trading partners around the world, it is vitally important to get the right advice BEFORE you go into any negotiations.

What is the role of UK Trading Standards and HM Customs and Excise?

Trading Standards in the UK and Her Majesty's Customs and Excise also play a vital part in policing the counterfeit trade in the UK; however, their resources are scarce and, thanks to woefully inadequate legal budgets, prosecutions are few and far between. Often the real impact of Trading Standards is through destroying computers owned by criminals and used for running their illegal business! My view, for what it is worth, is that brand owners should pay for private prosecutions in some instances, but again there is a reluctance to get involved in this type of enforcement. There is a bit of a "live and let live" attitude, which is naive and often damaging in my view.

What is the role of FAST, FACT and other trade organisations in deterring counterfeiting?

On the positive side, as well as trading standards, there are some excellent trade organisations out there that help IPR owners enforce their rights. As discussed previously in this book, these include the Federation against copyright theft or FACT and the Federation against Software Theft or FAST. Clearly the likes of Microsoft make a significant financial contribution to FAST that ultimately also helps other, smaller, software rights owners.

Let's not forget too that counterfeiting in the UK contributes a vaguely "respectable" front for a lot of seedy criminal activity such as drug running, money laundering and the trafficking of people. Chinese gangs bring individuals over to the UK to work in this slavish under world and the first thing they do is to take away an individual's identity and documents. The poor guy picked up by the police or Trading Standards officer in a raid on counterfeit DVD production in the UK is earning a pittance and sending what he can back home to keep his family fed. The police can arrest him and the Judge can order him to be deported but as I write this the Border Agency is powerless to deport him as they don't know who he actually is or where he's from! Without documents, he is simply released onto the streets and quite probably back to his old way of life – where else CAN he go? You'd do well to think about this when you are next offered knock-off DVDs or CDs in a pub or car boot sale.

This may sound like I'm simply knocking the Chinese – I'm not. There are lots of developing countries where counterfeiting arises; however, given the size and economic dynamics of China we shouldn't really be surprised at their position in the world of counterfeiting. As I said before, they are exploiting a business opportunity and making money out of what the West demands.

Counterfeiting vs look-alike goods

I'm often asked what the difference is between counterfeit goods, look-alikes and similar non-genuine products. Counterfeit goods are usually rip off goods to the last detail and also have trade marks and brands on them which the manufacturer doesn't own or have a licence for. As we've seen, they can even be goods from the same factory but are put on sale through unofficial channels. We associate them – wrongly in many instances – with car boot sales and similar routes to market. In fact, the biggest market place for them now is, of course, online. The sellers use the same sophisticated online marketing techniques as the brand owners themselves. Google ad word campaigns, Facebook pages, rip off websites, eBay– you name it, it can be scammed online. If you want to try this challenge for yourself, then Google terms such as 'luxury handbags', or 'designer handbags' and you'll see the extent of the problem.

In fairness many of the big online retailers such as eBay have vigorous enforcement policies. They will delist and black list sellers who trade in counterfeit products. The problem for brand owners is that as soon as one retailer is sent offline, another one pops up with a new website, or a Google ad campaign that directs traffic towards non-genuine goods. Since many of these sites are overseas, enforcement can be a problem. Some internet service providers (ISPs) are notoriously resistant in taking down rogue sites, although again ISPs based in the UK and search engines such as Google do take the issue very seriously indeed. They will act if formally notified and informed of offences.

Look a likes are more difficult to police. A pair of shoes for example can look like a designer brand, but in the absence of the original trade mark being attached and if the shoes aren't complete copies, then it is sometimes difficult to prosecute manufacturers; however, in some instances it is possible to pursue copied goods' makers under the common law of Passing Off. It is for this reason that so many retailers now do a roaring trade in items such as shoes, handbags and clothes that "look like" famous brands and designers. They're not. If all you're after is the look but not the build quality of the designer brand, then these could be for you. On the other hand poor quality copying is a problem. But as the advert goes if it doesn't have Kellogg's® on the box, it isn't Kellogg's® in the box. A killer slogan for Kellogg's® isn't it?

There are also the canny counterfeiters who put a registered trade mark ® on goods that are similar to but not identical with existing goods. So for example Nike® could be put on poor quality trainers, to dupe the purchaser into thinking they've bought a product which has a brand promise attached to it. I saw this first hand when a friend of mine inadvertently bought a non genuine Spyder® ski jacket. Now I purchased an original Spyder® jacket at great expense a few years ago. It has been superb, and I've never felt cold in it even when skiing at altitude in a blizzard, and it is brilliantly made. A friend of mine who bought an apparently genuine "Spyder" ski jacket "hardly worn" from the Internet found that it fell apart after one week's skiing! Putting a registered trade mark ® onto non genuine goods is a criminal act and the perpetrators of such deeds can face up to six months in prison. The trouble is that prosecutions by the Crown Prosecution Service are rare and brand owners are sometimes indifferent to customers' feedback.

The problem with counterfeiting

More sinister problems arise with counterfeit pharmaceuticals, aircraft parts or alcohol. These rip off copies can maim or kill. Again, manufacturers have a range of different methods of identifying genuine products, especially when it comes to pharmaceutical production. Packaging can be all important. Tamper proof cleverly labelled tablet boxes are commonly used in developed countries; however, there are still a lot of poor quality counterfeit drugs available, especially online. The sales and dispensing of drugs from online pharmacies in Europe is heavily regulated – in my experience the regulators rarely use the powers that they have. Some drugs such as Viagra and weight loss drugs are astonishingly easy to source, but many are poor quality copies from India and elsewhere and the amount of active ingredients and "fillers" can vary hugely. This can of course lead to very poor or a complete absence of clinical effects. The opposite is also true. The active ingredient in some counterfeit drugs can be so bioactive that they cause symptoms of overdose and in extreme cases substantial damage including liver failure etc.

There have also been numerous scandals in the past relating to aircraft parts. Whilst many of these incidents have arisen in the USA and former Soviet bloc countries, it is easy to see the economic drivers that foster this deadly trade. The airline industry, faced with mounting costs has sometimes been seduced by lower quality, none genuine aircraft parts. Bribery and corruption plays their part in the supply chain. Aircraft engineers and stores managers are not highly remunerated and in the past it has been far too easy for such personnel to make a bit on the side by buying fake rather than genuine replacement parts. Again the airline industry is now aware of the issues and most of the major airlines insist on genuine parts being used on aircraft and policing the supply chain to monitor the origins of various goods. Similar stories have also arisen in the car industry.

Counterfeit Alcohol

Last but not least is the trade in alcohol. It is estimated that in some parts of the world around 30% of all alcohol bought and sold is counterfeit. Take some methanol (industrial strength alcohol and very concentrated), add in some water and flavouring and, to the undiscerning, you have a drink such as vodka, rum or whisky depending on your added flavouring. Pure methanol is relatively easy and cheap to produce, add to this low production cost and easily copyable products versus high duty, high demand and sometimes high production cost for the genuine drink and you have the perfect storm for counterfeiting.

Fake bottles are sometime easy to acquire and unless the labelling and filling of the bottles is a challenge then it is quite easy to put fake product into circulation. But Methanol can kill people – especially if not properly diluted. Methanol poisoning can cause blindness – temporary and long term. It can also cause brain and liver damage. Take your pick – none of it sounds attractive to me.

Manufacturers and suppliers try and ensure that genuine products are labelled carefully with distinctive labels, holograms and special one way neck valves. High end French wines, so sought after by the Chinese market, do struggle with this. Some auction houses routinely smash bottles of wine after a tasting, yet, such bottles are readily available to the unscrupulous operator in China from restaurants and elsewhere, where they are re-filled with cheap poor quality plonk, re-corked and put back on sale!

Five key points to combat counterfeiting:

1. **Labelling, sales tags and certificates of origin.** It is now possible to use sophisticated labels and inks or even numbered certificates, which link your products to YOUR official production and sales routes. USE THEM!

2. **Think about the audit trail and production.** How can you monitor production and transport – especially where the goods are coming from a poorer country with low production costs? Also, consider moving manufacturing to the UK where controls can be much tighter.

3. **Invest in good local advice, local "minders" and management.** Have good local management and agents who look after YOUR interests.

4. **Be Vigilant with online sales.** Constantly monitor online presence for your trade mark and its use. Big companies such as BP have teams of people who monitor their online reputation for good reasons – scams abound. By way of example, those searching online for jobs can be led into thinking they're applying to big companies by unscrupulous online recruiters, also known as scammers, who use big brand logos to get job seekers to submit their CVs and a fee.

5. **Take action against infringers.** Invest in your defence. As Voltaire famously put it: "It is wise to kill an Admiral from time to time to encourage the others." So take out the big players and watch the smaller counterfeiters move to another easier to rip off target.

And Finally...The Future Looks Bright

This book has taken me what seems like ages to write and whilst you may think there is a lot in it, there's far more I could write. If I've increased your awareness of the issues, benefits and potential pitfalls around intellectual property, then I've succeeded in my mission. At the time of concluding this book in early 2014 I'm optimistic about the future of the UK. As we begin to climb out of the recent recession we have a bright future to look forward to through our ingenuity and our technology. There are numerous Government schemes to help us too – look at Growth Accelerator at www.growthaccelerator.com for starters.

Lots of my clients are making money from exporting – the recent recession causing them to look overseas for new customers. I do genuinely believe that British businesses have woken up to many of the mistakes they've made in the past. We are not shackled to history and outdated work practices as some countries are. We are not taxing talented individuals out of existence, and our current corporation taxes, R&D tax regime and Patent Box schemes are causing an inward flow of investment. As is the fact that actually quite a lot of business people from China, Brazil, Russia and elsewhere, quite like living here – we're an easy and good place to live and do business. The UK is a place where everyone can live in a fair society. Investors can and will invest and we will all prosper. Our employment laws mean that employees, whilst well protected, are not impossible to get rid of. Our justice system is, by and large, fair and free from corruption and we have specialist courts, which operate as they should! We forget that on a worldwide stage these issues are important to people and are VERY important to businesses. It is people who make business happen. Business people look for certainty when making decisions and, as such, we're a great place to operate from!

Finally, when the UK came out of a deep recession back in the 1970s, its reserves of North Sea oil served its balance of payments well. Sadly, much of the bonanza has been wasted by successive Governments; however in 2014, the UK is using a range of UK based scientific experts in fracking technology – obtaining long term gas supplies from shale rock beneath our feet, a workable reality. Experts predict that if properly managed, our gas supplies will be assured for many years to come and the cost of gas and therefore power will plummet. This has to be good news for industry and for the UK generally. Further evidence, if it were needed that our scientists, brand owners, engineers, software designers, musicians and technologists do deliver world class performance. Let's make a collective effort to keep them world class!

About the Author

First and I think foremost, I'm a scientist. Things that make life easier, that whizz, bang, change colour or explode still fascinate me. How a human body works is a constant source of amazement to me. So is the natural world. That is why after my first degree in Genetics and Cell Biology I spent the first 10 years of my career in the health and care industry (big pharma as they say in the trade). In that time during the 1980s the pharma industry came out with an abundant pipeline of new drugs to treat everything from Aids to diabetes. New surgical techniques such as keyhole surgery and the use of scanners, lasers and diathermy revolutionised medical treatments, as did advances in wound care and anaesthetics. In 1992 I decided to have a change of direction and retrain my analytical mind to become a lawyer.

Since qualification in the mid-1990s I've specialised in intellectual property. Again, this area of law fascinates me, dealing as it does with technology (often but not always patented), brands, know-how, databases, copyrights, design rights and rights of confidence. Since qualification I've worked for large national and international law firms, becoming an expert in my field and I've lectured to other lawyers on my subject.

I realised fairly quickly that most lawyers in private practice are driven by their own internal targets and agenda and lacked real commercial expertise and objectivity, hence I set up my own firm in 2007 in order to look out for clients and not inwards for internal rewards. Today, I run my own specialist practice – a regulated law firm of solicitors that creates strategy, wealth and value for my clients out of their good ideas; their intellectual property.

My intention was and is to create a practice with a real difference and true insight into WHAT and WHY something creates value. To me other law firms don't see the commercial value of what their clients have created, or they simply conduct themselves in a reactive rather than proactive manner. In order to unearth the crown jewels in any business it is really important to work differently. Quite a number of other professionals – including some solicitors, barristers and patent or trade mark attorneys won't like some of the things I say in this book, but frankly, as Rhett so eloquently put it, "I don't give a damn", I think business has been further badly served on some occasions by these people and I won't shirk from saying so. Please learn, enjoy and pass it on.

Index